MULTICULTURAL DYNAMICS
AND THE ENDS OF HISTORY

MULTICULTURAL DYNAMICS AND THE ENDS OF HISTORY

EXPLORING KANT, HEGEL, AND MARX

Réal Fillion

LIBRARY AND ARCHIVES CANADA CATALOGUING IN PUBLICATION

Fillion, Réal Robert, 1963-
    Multicultural dynamics and the ends of history : exploring Kant, Hegel, and Marx / Réal Fillion.

(Philosophica, ISSN 1480-4670)
Includes bibliographical references and index.
ISBN 978-0-7766-0670-5

    1. History--Philosophy. 2. Multiculturalism--Philosophy. 3. Kant,
    Immanuel, 1724-1804. 4. Hegel, Georg Wilhelm Friedrich, 1770-1831.
    5. Marx, Karl, 1818-1883. I. Title. II. Series: Collection Philosophica

D16.8.F46 2008   901   C2007-907280-1

Published by the University of Ottawa Press, 2008
542 King Edward Avenue
Ottawa, Ontario K1N 6N5
www.uopress.uottawa.ca

The University of Ottawa Press acknowledges with gratitude the support extended to its publishing list by Heritage Canada through its Book Publishing Industry Development Program, by the Canada Council for the Arts, by the Canadian Federation for the Humanities and Social Sciences through its Aid to Scholarly Publications Program, by the Social Sciences and Humanities Research Council, and by the University of Ottawa. We also gratefully acknowledge the University of Sudbury's financial support towards the publication of this book.

Pour Annie, Maxime et Magali

Acknowledgements

Though essentially a solitary activity, the project of writing this book was nevertheless sustained by others. I would like to thank those closest to me, Annie, Maxime (for seeing and suggesting Paul Gauguin's masterpiece for the cover) and Magali (for leaving little notes of encouragement on my desk) but also my brother, Gabriel, who read through an early draft. Thanks also to Michael Yeo for stimulating conversations in the car, and the M.A. in the Humanities at Laurentian University for the opportunity to present some of these ideas. Thanks to Peter Saunders for his help in the process of finding a publisher and for his encouragement. The comments of the reviewers of the University of Ottawa Press were generous and very helpful. Thanks to Eric Nelson of the University of Ottawa Press and, especially, to Alex Anderson for his enthusiasm and his very efficient handling of the production process. I would like to acknowledge the University of Sudbury for its support. I gratefully acknowledge the journal *History and Theory*, Wesleyan University and Blackwell Publishing for the permission to use parts of my article "Moving Beyond Biopower: Hardt and Negri's Post-Foucauldian Speculative Philosophy of History," *History and Theory Theme Issue* 44 (December, 2005), 47-72. This book has been published with the help of a grant from the Canadian Federation for the Humanities and Social Sciences, through the Aid to Scholarly Publications Program, using funds provided by the Social Sciences and Humanities Research Council of Canada.

Table of Contents

Preface

The primary purpose of this book is to show the relevance of speculative philosophy of history, in both classical and contemporary forms, as a framework for thinking about the following broad question: given the various developments taking place throughout the world, with specific reference to its increasingly multicultural character, where are we headed?

Responding to such a question requires that we rearticulate a sense of the movement of history as a developmental whole. This has been the traditional concern of speculative philosophy of history. By exploring the classical figures of Immanuel Kant, Georg Wilhelm Friedrich Hegel, and Karl Marx, and particular ways in which these figures are taken up today, I show how we can discern in our increasingly multicultural world both what I call the *dynamics* of history (what moves history forward) and the *telos* of history (its end or goal). More specifically, I argue that examining the speculative philosophies of history of Kant, Hegel, and Marx helps us better understand the *relation* between the dynamics and the telos of history.

This is a somewhat risky move on my part, given that the speculative philosophy of history is no longer very well-regarded within the philosophical community, largely because of our contemporary preoccupation with specialized knowledge. This term "speculative" is usually used to distinguish those philosophical accounts whose concern is with the whole of history and the questions that arise from considering history as a whole, such as: does history have a meaning? Does it move progressively? Or cyclically? Does it determine the fate of human beings? Or can human beings direct its course by their actions? It is usually contrasted with what has come to be called "analytic" philosophy of history (sometimes also called "critical" philosophy of history). This latter approach eschews such speculative efforts, considers them unfounded (and, well, speculative), and prefers instead to examine questions that relate more specifically to the issue of the kind of knowledge that historical investigations can be said to yield. The questions that such a philosophical approach considers concern whether or not historical knowledge can be considered "objective" (given that the object, the past, no longer exists); whether or not historians can be impartial in their treatment of the facts (given that they themselves are implicated in the thing they are attempting to describe); and whether or not history needs to be written as a narrative or should express its findings in other formats.

The rejection by analytic philosophers of history of speculative philosophy of history is an interesting story that I cannot engage in here (at least not directly, though questions relative to that story will be raised along the way), but that rejection has been quite widespread, given the relative scarcity of speculative philosophers of history. Indeed, the speculative philosophies of history that I shall be discussing were written in the late eighteenth and nineteenth centuries.

One of the reasons that there are fewer speculative philosophies of history is that our knowledge of the past, the knowledge generated by the work of countless historians, has grown exponentially, leading to a certain wariness towards any claim pretending to encapsulate the whole of history. I certainly share in that wariness. However, the point of a speculative philosophy of history, as I understand it, is not to *encapsulate* the whole of history, but to attempt to *think* it *as* a whole. This I think is reasonable and doable, and it is precisely such attempts to find the conceptual means to think history as a whole that one finds in the speculative efforts that I shall be considering.

I recognize that many readers may remain sceptical of the pertinence of such a project, especially given that I have announced that I shall be discussing the philosophy of history of, among others, Karl Marx. Conventional wisdom would have it that, if anything has been thoroughly discredited today, given the course of twentieth-century history, it is the conception of history that animated Marxism. Without engaging in polemics, I would like then to consider briefly what the speculative philosophy of history is not, or can no longer be (if it ever was).

Maurice Lagueux has argued, in his recent book *Actualité de la philosophie de l'histoire*, that speculative philosophy of history, far from being irrelevant, is in fact a privileged locus for making sense of the events that occur in history. When sociologists, political theorists, and other social commentators try to make sense of current events, they are effectively engaged in a very similar activity and are motivated by the same concerns as speculative philosophers of history. Lagueux's work is interesting in that he shows how those who wish to distinguish their attempts to make sense of current events from the speculative efforts of philosophers of history can be seen to have a very specific view of what speculative philosophy of history is. Lagueux identifies this view in terms of five characteristics that are said to mar the speculative efforts of philosophers of history (Lagueux pp. 171–181):

(1) a disdain for facts;

(2) a presumed knowledge of the future;

(3) dogmatism;

(4) an insistence on teleology; and

(5) the presumption to give the meaning of history understood as a whole.

I would like to examine briefly these five characteristics. I do not want to evaluate whether they adequately reflect the actual works of speculative philosophers of history, though I do not believe that they do, and they certainly do not capture the force and significance of the works of Kant, Hegel or Marx. Here I want merely to distinguish *my* concern with speculative philosophy of history from these presumed drawbacks.

First, then, I address the presumed disdain for facts exhibited by speculative philosophy of history. Certainly, one should never disdain facts. However, facts themselves are always articulated within an overall understanding that frames them and gives them their relevance as *the* facts of a given situation. With regard to the use of facts, speculative philosophy of history is often accused of selecting only those facts that accord with a predetermined understanding of what is actually happening in the world. For example, if what I mean to say when I say that the world is "becoming increasingly multicultural" is that the world is increasingly recognizing the equal status and worth of the various cultures that are increasingly in contact, and in support of this assertion I select only those facts that in effect support this view, while purposely ignoring other facts that demonstrate the opposite, such as increased conflict and intolerance, then I would be engaging in the kind of speculative thinking that is, rightly, criticized.

Of course, the problem is not with the selection of facts itself. Selection is inevitable and necessary, and the relevance of what one is saying depends on it. The problem arises when the selection ignores what, given that selection, it should consider, such as the fact that cultural contact takes on many forms, not all of which will be compatible. Yet this is not a problem particular to the philosophy of history. It inheres in any attempt to make sense of complex realities.

What is perhaps more interesting and more pertinent to the philosophy of history are the *kinds* of facts that get selected. Paul Veyne, an important historian of Roman antiquity who has written about the epistemology of history and historiography in his book *Writing History: Essay on Epistemology*, calls historical facts, the facts that historians deal with, "sublunar" facts, in order to distinguish them from the facts that are framed within the natural sciences, and are meant to provide support for the formulation of laws in terms of constancy and necessity. Veyne's point, of course, is that the human historical world, the "sublunar" world, does not display the kind of constancy and regularity that the starry heavens display, and that appealing to its "facts" must reflect this if such appeals are to be reflective of that world. The appeal to facts in scientific explanation becomes, in historical investigations of the human world, the *explication* of factors that contribute to our ability to make sense of human affairs. We move, then, from "facts" to "factors," which, according to Veyne, can be distinguished into three different kinds. Explicating any human situation will need to take into consideration, certainly, the material conditions within which it takes place, but consideration must also be given to human deliberations, and to the ways in which they modulate those conditions, which themselves are subject to chance and happenstance. All of these factors are to be found within the establishment of the "facts" of the human historical world, and it is these "facts" that speculative philosophy of history should be careful not to disdain when it considers history as a whole.

The challenge that recognition of our "sublunar" condition poses for speculative philosophy of history is that, when we think of history as a whole, we must remember how these different factors play off one another. That is, when we consider history as a whole, what I shall be calling the past-present-future complex, we are not to consider it as governed by overarching laws, for this would be to overlook human deliberation, as well as chance and happenstance. Nor are we to consider it as the senseless product of mere chance, for this would be to overlook the ends devised by human deliberation in response to material conditions. Nor are we to think of history as necessarily directed towards a deliberatively constituted end, for this would be to overlook the force of material conditions, as well as chance and happenstance. Rather, speculative philosophy of history must be respectful of those facts that help us explicate our involvement in the world as it unfolds.

The second characteristic identified by Lagueux is the presumed knowledge of the future that it is often thought speculative philosophies of history proclaim. If speculative philosophies of history include the future in their consideration, it is because the future forms a part of the human historical world, or, as I shall call it, of the past-present-future complex. In particular, as we shall see, consideration of the future will most often get expressed through consideration of how the *ideal* relates to the *real*. Such considerations of the future are, of course, implicit in-the basic question motivating this investigation: where are we headed, given the increasingly multicultural character of the world? No knowledge of the future is presumed here, only concern for it.

The third and fourth characteristics identified by Lagueux, namely the presumed dogmatism and teleological insistences of speculative philosophies of history, need to be dealt with together because the criticism of speculative philosophies of history results from their combination: an end of history, towards which history is ineluctably moving, is dogmatically affirmed. A dogmatic affirmation of what the end or telos of history is cannot be compatible with any *philosophical* attempt to make sense of history. Philosophy is *essentially* a questioning activity and does not typically result in dogmatic pronouncements.

This is not to say that the articulation of the end or telos of history is without merit. On the contrary, much of this work is devoted to considering the relevance of such articulations insofar as they help us respond to our question. When a telos is ascribed to history, it is usually because there is an attempt to think history as a whole, that is, to consider the past, the present, and the future as a single *process*. To think of the past, the present, and the future as a process is to assume or presume that the past, the present, and the future cohere in an intelligible way or in certain discernable ways. A particular way of describing that coherence is to say that this process is *directed*, that it can, as a process, be seen to be moving in a particular direction, or in a particular directed fashion. When this kind of speculative move is made, two questions might be said to arise.

The first question concerns what the direction is, which often gets specified by asking what is the endpoint or destination that (ultimately) governs the direction. This is the *teleological* question: it asks what is the end or telos of this process called history. A second question concerns what *drives* the process such that it is directed in the way that it is. One might be tempted to call this question the "causal" one, but that might lead one to think that the process of history needs to be understood as deriving from something outside history, whereas part of the point of these speculative efforts is to account for this process from within history. It would be more accurate to call this question the question of the *dynamics* of history: what, if anything, can be said to *move* history, to be the motor of history? The different approaches to both the *telos* and the *dynamics* of history, as these get articulated in the classical speculative philosophies of history, will be the primary focus of this book.

Kant sets the stage in Part I by identifying the *telos* of history as the full development of our natural capacities, something that is, paradoxically, achieved through the conflictual dynamics of the "unsocial sociability" of human beings. While important for identifying how history can be seen as a developmental whole, Kant's "cosmopolitan" understanding of the dynamics of history will ultimately be shown to be too abstract to help us respond concretely to the question of where *we* are headed. Indeed, much of the subsequent story of the development of speculative philosophy of history can be read, particularly if one focuses on Hegel and Marx as I propose to, as the attempt to give Kant's telos historical form and content, an attempt to concretize the abstract ideal that it articulates.

Part II explores how the theme of recognition inspired by Hegel's understanding of the dynamics of history shows more concretely how such an ideal is realized. Such a theme is especially relevant to a world that is increasingly becoming multicultural. However, the dynamics of mutual recognition that move history forward are able to create only limited spaces of what I call "reasonability." Although they are crucial to social life, such spaces leave too much human suffering outside the scope of the historical "realization of reason."

Part III argues that Marx's identification of the basic struggle within history as between those exploited in the interests of a few versus those whose interests are realized in common is the most promising account of how to understand the link between the dynamics of history and its telos or goal, which, for Marx, is the free development of the productive and creative capacities of all, especially if we consider the increasingly multicultural dimension of our living and working together.

Thus my basic claim is that, if the discussion of the *telos* and its articulation to the *dynamics* of history is what best characterizes classical speculative philosophy of history, and that this distinguishes it from those other non-philosophical characteristics that Lagueux identified, which we can sum up as *the dogmatic assertion of knowledge of the future that disdains consideration of the facts of human history*, then a case can be made for the relevance of speculative philosophy of history for helping us respond to the speculative question of where we are headed.

This brings me to Lagueux's final characteristic of speculative philosophy of history, namely, providing the meaning or significance of history considered as a whole. Lagueux is quite right to point out that the interrogation of the sense or significance of historical events is something that engages the intellectual effort of countless people, from social scientists to social activists and, of course, historians, and that it hardly makes sense to fault philosophers of history for engaging in it as well. The objection, therefore, cannot be directed at the investigation of the sense or meaning of history, but must rather be aimed at the claim of speculative philosophers of history to be investigating the sense or meaning of history *as a whole*. It seems to me that the proper response to such an objection is to point out that, while it is true that our specialized knowledges, by their very nature and structures, cannot yield answers to these preoccupations with the overall unfolding of our world, this does not mean that such preoccupations are unreasonable: where, indeed, are we headed? Because such preoccupations are not unreasonable, we should not be surprised when something other than such knowledges responds to them. Speculative philosophies, as I shall attempt to show, are very respectful of our specialized knowledges, and indeed have contributed to them, and in that sense they are important allies in our general attempt to make better sense of our lives and our world. They do not *oppose* our specialized knowledges. What they supply, I shall be arguing, is the basic *hopefulness* that undergirds and maintains our combined efforts to make *better* sense of the world. Even though such hopefulness animates on a daily basis most of the activities we undertake (why else do we go on?), we are only intermittently conscious of it and appreciative of its necessity in sustaining the conditions for the living of truly human lives. The following speculative effort is an attempt to respond to that intermittence by shoring up this essential hopefulness, a hopefulness that can become clouded by the feelings of senselessness that often surface and spread when such speculations either fade or fail.

Where Are We Headed?

This book attempts to work out a philosophical response to two general preoccupations that, I believe, characterize our time. These preoccupations can be felt more as nagging feelings than as explicitly articulated thoughts. One of the reasons for writing this work is to give articulation to such feelings, which I share with my contemporaries. I believe that this is a principal professional task of those of us who do philosophy. (Like most of us who "do philosophy" professionally, I am a professor at a university, a faculty member of a philosophy department.)

The first preoccupation, I think, can be expressed most clearly in the form of a question, which for the moment I shall express as generally as possible. The question asks: where are we headed? It is a question we ask, or a feeling that nags at us, when, for example, we watch the news and are made to follow "developments" that are clearly working themselves out, but whose goals and outcomes are far from clear. The most prominent example that comes to mind as I write this is the occupation of Iraq. Other examples might include the Israeli–Palestinian conflict, global warming, the consolidation of the European Union, the threat of an avian-flu pandemic and biotechnological developments, but the list could be continued indefinitely. The point I wish to make is that when we are made to think about the "world" —the "state of the world," as it were—we are confronted with various developments, situations that are evolving and changing as we confront them and try to make sense of them. Confronting these various developments considered as a whole can give rise to a distinct feeling of discomfort, a nagging feeling that demands attention and that I am suggesting should be articulated in the form of the question: where, given all of these developments that confront us, are we headed?

This is a very general question and, in this age of specialized knowledge, it is hard for most of us to see how one might go about answering it. The first thing I need to do is to argue for the legitimacy of general questions even when no answers are immediately forthcoming. I say this to forestall what might be a typical response to the question as I have articulated it: to turn away from it *because* of its generality. All the developments that confront us arise out of complex conditions that can be, and indeed are, analyzed and thoughtfully considered by many knowledgeable persons, whose opinions are sometimes canvassed within the presentation of those developments. They may not be able to answer the *general* question of "where we are headed," but they can and do answer specific questions about what is happening right now and what is likely to happen next: a timetable for the withdrawal of Coalition troops from Iraq, or an increase in their numbers; measures taken to prepare for the spread of the avian-flu virus, which include developing vaccination programs; interpretations of what the Kyoto Protocol demands of its signatories. However, the point I wish to make is that these specific and specialized answers to specific questions do not *replace* the more general question of "where we are headed," which articulates the very real feeling of discomfort that arises when these developments are considered *as a whole*.

Now, it might be argued by those dispensing specialized responses to specialized questions that my more general question is not a *real* question. It may, or may not, address what I have been calling a "nagging feeling" about the "state of the world" in its various developments, but it does not actually articulate a real *question*, precisely because the question as posed does not admit of an answer. Or rather, the response to a question such as "where are we headed?" can only be an emphatic: we do not know.

I think this is an appropriate thing to say. Indeed, we do not know where we are headed and, if anyone claims to *know* where we are headed, they are mistaken. No one has available to him or her any general *knowledge* of what will happen in the future. Of course, this lack of knowledge does not prevent us from predicting, from our experience of the past, what is *likely* to happen, given present conditions. However, the accuracy of those predictions will depend on how well we understand our past experiences and our present conditions. All of which seems to be an argument for turning to those specialized responses to specialized questions about past experiences and present conditions in order to understand the developments that confront us, as opposed to wasting our time asking questions that cannot be answered.

Many readers will no doubt have noticed that I have insisted on the term "developments." I have done this to draw attention to the typical way the "world" is presented to us (think of the news on television). It is presented, not as a static state of affairs, but as a dynamic whole that is unfolding in certain determinate ways. That the world is treated as a developing whole that unfolds reflects an assumption we make about the world. The assumption that the world is *dynamic and unfolding* reveals itself in the way we think that the decisions and actions that are undertaken today will impact in specific if only relatively predictable ways on what happens tomorrow. The assumption that the world is a *whole* reveals itself in our insistence on presenting things happening at great distances from each other as being relevant to one another.

The reason I point this out is that both the "nagging feeling" and the question of where we are headed address themselves less to the (in this case relative lack of) *knowledge* we have about the world, than to the *assumptions* we make about it, as these are revealed in the way we present it to ourselves. In particular, it addresses the assumption we make about the world as being a *developmental whole*.

This book is primarily concerned with that assumption and how examining it can help relieve the "nagging feeling" that accompanies it. Its response to the question "where are we headed?" will propose less an answer than a way of thinking through or making sense of the question itself. In other words, it will provide a *philosophical* response to the question, which is something different from a specialized answer to a specialized question.

I mentioned at the beginning of this introduction *two* general preoccupations that motivated this philosophical investigation. The first preoccupation I have described as our preoccupation with how we are to situate ourselves within the world seen as a developing whole. The second preoccupation I shall articulate, not in terms of a question, but rather in terms of a twin set of observations about the world that many people make, or to which many people are prepared to agree. Those observations are that the world "is increasingly becoming multicultural" and "the world is increasingly becoming one world." As with the question "where are we headed?" my aim is to deal with these observations philosophically. That is, I am not here concerned with what might be called the *empirical* validity of the observation that the world is becoming increasingly multicultural, which would involve developing ways to measure whether or not the world is indeed becoming more "multicultural," perhaps by means of statistical data concerning immigration, patterns of settlement and resettlement, and retention of distinct cultural practices. Rather, my concern is to examine the way in which these observations reveal certain assumptions we make about the world, and how these assumptions contribute to shaping the world in particular ways. My argument will be that examining the assumptions revealed by these observations will help us make better sense of the question of where we are headed, which I believe is an important question to which we not only *can* respond, but *are* indeed responding, in ways that can be made more explicit.

This can be illustrated if we look more carefully at the twin set of observations that the world is becoming increasingly multicultural and that the world is becoming increasingly one world. On the surface, these two observations appear to be in conflict. An increasingly multicultural world is, presumably, one that manifests increasing diversity. But then in what sense is the world becoming increasingly one?

One way to deal with the apparent conflict is to recognize that we are dealing with very general observations taken from different vantage points: a view from the ground, as it were, and a view from above. On the ground, diversity is manifest. All around us there are different cultures, different ways of going about one's way, different ways of making sense of things. From above, however, what one observes is the shared space of a single world. Things may be unequally distributed within that shared space, but it nevertheless remains shared: a blue planet harbouring, and threatening, many forms of life.

Although these two vantage points offer very different perspectives, it should be noted that the expression "our multicultural world" seems to want to hold on to both at the same time. Our (one) world is a multicultural (one). To say that our world is multicultural is already to say that it is not "one" in any simple, straightforward sense, but, at the same time, to say that ours is a multicultural *world* is to give a kind of unified sense to that diversity.

On the ground, then, what we might be said to observe is increasing diversity. By "observe" I mean the rather involved activity of thinking that involves seeing things against a background of other things, understanding how those things relate to each other and to my observing them, and the expectations that follow from such understanding, among other things. That is, to observe something is already to place it within a pre-existing framework of reference constructed out of patterns of inference and modes of assertion (as Robert B. Brandom explains in his *Making It Explicit: Reasoning, Representing, and Discursive Commitment*). To say that what one observes is an increasing diversity is to say that the assertions that one makes, the inferences that one draws, and the references that one appeals to all contain elements of the unfamiliar along with the more regular familiarities of one's thinking.

Let me develop the following example to illustrate how the recognition of diversity in terms of relative familiarities impacts on how one thinks about one's world. It is not uncommon today to encounter in one's daily activities persons speaking a language that one does not understand. One may be familiar enough with features of the language to identify it as, say, Spanish, Urdu or Swahili without, however, understanding what is being said. Now, what I want to suggest and consider is that such an encounter, say, on the bus on the way home from work, within the context or logical space—the context within which we refer, infer and assert features of the world around us—recognized as that of an "increasingly multicultural world," has distinctive features. For one, the speakers of the uncomprehended language, which may perhaps be not altogether unfamiliar, in the sense that one may indeed be able to identify the language itself, are not necessarily considered by the listener who does not understand the language to be foreigners, or not, that is, by the listener who has observed and accepts that we live in an "increasingly multicultural world," though he or she might assert that the speakers are speaking a foreign language.

Now, the point I wish to draw attention to is that this willingness to distinguish the speaker from the speech is quite remarkable, when one thinks about it as it arises from a specifically constructed social situation. Because our use of language is so connected to our identities, it is not surprising that, for a very long time, identifying one's speech was at the same time identifying the speaker. However, what our "increasingly multicultural world" is revealing is that the relation between speaker and speech is much more involved and layered than this ready identification implies. Of course, persons who regularly speak more than one language have always been aware of this complexity, which can be the cause of considerable existential angst, as the French-speaking, English-writing author of this book can testify. In fact, what our "increasingly multicultural world" in part signifies is the increasingly widespread acknowledgement of the constructed and revisable character of the identification of speaker and speech, largely because more and more people go through their lives speaking more than one language on a regular basis.

Let us return to the example of the bus ride. A group of people are speaking a language that I acknowledge is foreign to me, but obviously not to them, which means, in an "increasingly multicultural world," that I am prepared to restrict my ascription of "foreignness" to the language and not to the speakers themselves. Of course, the speakers may actually *be* foreigners, that is, tourists visiting the city and riding on public transportation. This might be made evident in a number of ways: they might be looking with some animation out the window, and pointing to persons and things; cameras may be strung around their necks and guides to the city may be sticking out of their pockets. My point, however, is that, absent these additional markers, in an "increasingly multicultural world" we would not be justified in ascribing the status of foreigners to speakers of a foreign language whom one encounters on the bus. Indeed, this would be a kind of mistake, a kind of failure on our part to acknowledge the true character of our surrounding circumstances, something like a "hasty generalization" as identified by the canons of informal logic. I mean this reference to a *logical* mistake in a strong sense. In a social space that is openly and "increasingly" understood to be multicultural, to fail to distinguish between speaker and speech is to fail to understand the normative and logical parameters of that space.

This, of course, is merely an example of the kinds of considerations that can arise if we accept the assertion that the world is "increasingly becoming multicultural." Many more of these considerations will be discussed in due course. The general introductory point I would like to emphasize is that asserting or affirming that the world is "becoming increasingly multicultural" is asserting or affirming that the world is in fact *changing*, and that making sense of the world must take this fact into consideration. It is by attending to the fact of a *changing world* that we can better understand how the assertion that the world is "becoming increasingly multicultural" links up with the question of "where we are headed."

In order to see this more clearly, I would like to refine the question of "where we are headed" by adding a prefatory clause: "given the way the world presents itself to us, where are we headed?" No doubt the reader can see where I am going with this clause: namely, that the world presents itself as "increasingly multicultural." However, to get the full sense of what is involved here, these preliminary and more general considerations are required.

There are two components to this question that need to be clarified straight off. The first concerns the notion that the world is something that presents itself to us. The second concerns the reference to a "we."

The way I understand the two components is that the first articulates the philosophical generality of the question, whereas the second seeks to ground this generality in a specific context (*where* "we" are headed). The point I wish to make by posing the question in this way is to show that attention to the different "ways in which the world presents itself to us" actually shows how we are indeed always headed somewhere within it. In fact, that is what it *means* to say that the world presents itself to us in a particular way.

Let me give an example. When you wake up, you wake up to a particular world. The world presents itself to you in a particular way, perhaps at first as a beeping alarm clock, or sunlight on your face, or a small child tugging on your sleeve, or the kneading of a cat's paws, or a kiss from a partner's mouth. Whatever the case may be, the way the world presents itself to you is at the same time descriptive of your orientation within it. That is, as it presents itself to you, you also make your way through and within it. Your hand strikes the alarm clock, landing on the snooze button with remarkable precision, and your eyes verify the time displayed, confirming that you need not get out of bed immediately, though soon enough. The warm sun on your face lets you wake up more slowly, perhaps contemplating the leisurely day ahead or, less fortunately, you sit bolt upright and turn with panic to the traitorous alarm clock, curses bursting out of you as you scramble out of bed. Waking up to the world every morning is also being directed within it, which means, for those likely to be reading these lines, probably first to a washroom, then some breakfast, then work or leisure.

Simply pointing this out, however, and with fairly little effort, one can imagine very different worlds, implying very different orientations upon awakening: dangerous worlds, perhaps, unrecognized worlds, worlds with no immediate prospect of nourishment or employment, worlds with little choice, worlds with too much choice. I leave it to the reader's imagination to work out the details (a useful exercise), but I would point out that, whatever the world, it is one in which one's bearings are taken and that one either heads into or hides from.

It is within this very general understanding of the ways in which the world presents itself to us that I ask the more specific question of where *we* are headed. Where are *we* headed in the world, given the ways in which it presents itself to us? That is my question.

Note that I have now pluralized the "ways" in which the world presents itself to us. This is because we are getting more specific, more concrete. There will be different and competing ways of specifying the general point.

The "we" at this point needs to be understood as inclusively as possible, referring to all who are indeed headed somewhere within the world presented to them, which, I suggest, means all those who depend on a sense of this orientation within the world. Ultimately, however, "we" means all of us, everyone, all human beings, and, interestingly, not only those presently alive, but *all* human beings, past, present, and future, so long as there is a world presenting itself. Such a "we" is, of course, difficult to think about clearly, or concretely, but actually it is not as difficult as one may initially assume. The trick is not to fly off too quickly into a generalized "we," such as "humanity," or even "human beings," because these latter categories tend to take on a life of their own and replace the concrete "we" at issue. We would do better to stick closer to the ground and think about how "we" spread ourselves over space and time.

First, time. I often ask my students if they know their grandmother's maiden name. Many do. When it comes to *her* mother's maiden name, however, they are utterly at a loss, and often not because they are unable to recall it, but because they were never introduced to it. That generation of their families has never been presented to them, though the very mention of one's grandmother's mother makes her now appear, however nebulously. This, by the way, is where budding historians can be identified: the nebulous appearance of figures of the past is intriguing to some people, provoking a desire to investigate how to render these figures more real, which can be as simple as asking simple questions of one's grandmother about her mother, which of course can lead to other evocations of the past, so that all of a sudden the world takes on a different hue. Even for those who are not historians, such genealogical links are of course a way of linking ourselves in the present to our past.

However, we do not merely want to stay within the familial sphere: after all, families develop and renew themselves through their encounters with extra-familial others (as we shall discuss later). Even if we do restrict ourselves to that sphere, it is not long before we move beyond those genealogical linkages that connect us "directly" to those nebulous, though named, figures of the past. We want to look out also to the world that sustained and, perhaps, mangled those lives linked to our own. What did the world look like to them? How did it present itself to them when they opened their eyes in the morning?

My own grandparents were born in the 1890s, at about the same time as the automobile, though none of them traveled in one until they were adults. I mention this because my ten-year- old son is fascinated with cars, which of course are all around him. He was both amused and puzzled by the provenance of the term "horsepower." It is hard to imagine and understand how a wagon pulled by 265 horses is meant to represent the power and performance of the vehicle that (he wishes) his father drove. Of course, the notion of a horse's strength was much more familiar to his great-grandfather, who used both horses and tractors in his lifetime. The world has changed a great deal over the past one hundred years. Indeed, consideration of these changes, and of the speed with which things continue to change, is a prime motivation for considering our question: where are we headed?

In order to think about these changes and the different directions they allow or forestall, we shall need to make use of a number of concepts. Right now we are trying to make sense of the concept of "we." We have noticed that it does not take long to realize that a "we" that rather straightforwardly includes members of our families (grandparents and their parents) involves us in the task of thinking very different worlds, such as, in the example given above, a world in which the concept of horsepower is introduced to one where its etymology needs to be explained.

Making sense of these different worlds involves making use of the concepts of the past, the present, and the future. We use the past, and what we know of the past, to make sense of the concept of "horsepower" as it presents itself to us in the present, as one of the specifications that entice us to purchase this or that particular model of automobile, and at the same time points to the future. Increased horsepower involves the consumption of increased amounts of fuel, which, for the time being, is produced from non-renewable resources available only under certain kinds of highly complex organized conditions.

We have seen that the world presents itself to us in such a way that we orient ourselves within it. We have also seen that that presentation has a temporal dimension, that is, it involves the past, the present, and the future. When we talk about the world in terms of the fact that it has a past, a present, and a future, we are talking about an *historical* world. In more technical language, we are talking about the *historicity* of the world. The world presents itself to us in such a way that it includes and involves a reference to the past, the present, and the future. I shall attempt to keep this discussion as free of technical language as possible, not because there is something wrong with technical language (it is often required in order to get certain kinds of job done), but because I am not asking a technical question. I am asking a *philosophical* question about what we might be able to think and say about where we are headed, given the way that the world presents itself to us. We haven't gotten too far yet, but we are moving forward.

If the world presents itself to us *historically*, that is, involves us in considerations of the past, the present, and the future, we need to work out how we should understand how these different tenses relate to each other. We begin with the past.

Evidence of the past is everywhere around us, of course. Just think of historical buildings that, by their architectural distinctiveness, call up different ways of conceiving both lived space and what the eye should see. The simple point I would like to make here is that our involvement in and with the past, both in terms of what we remember of the past and of what we have forgotten, is precisely that of relating to the world as it presents itself, as *evidence* of what is in the world, indeed of what the world *is* both in terms of what it offers us to understand, and what it allows us to do with that understanding. Another way of saying this is that, whatever evidence we consider in the present (or better: at present) actually *comes from the past*. The evidence we consider, although we do so in the present, does not come from the present, is not produced by the present, but literally comes from something *other* than the present: it comes from the past. What I want to insist on is this is what the past *is*: it is the evidence of the world that the present considers. If I relate this consideration to our initial question, then it tells us that, when we are contemplating where we are headed, given the way the world presents itself to us, any appeal to the evidence that the world provides is an appeal to the past.

I am even prepared to go further and suggest that, whenever, in our response to our initial question, we make use of the notion of *knowledge*, we are making use of the past, of the pastness of the world, if you like, as it presents itself. This sounds a lot like playing with words, but it is not. The world considered as evidence is the relational contribution of the past to our experience of it. The pastness of the world is the world presenting itself to us as evidence of itself.

Of course, this sounds very abstract, but that is because we are considering matters very generally. That is why it is important not to forget the initial question that remains our guide. To be able to respond to the question of where we are headed, we need to orient ourselves within the world that presents itself to us in specific ways. Right now we are considering how it presents itself to us as *evidence*. It does so by showing how the world arises out of the past.

Here is an example. I hear a sound I don't immediately recognize. I ask myself what the sound is, which is in fact remembering what the sound might have been, by placing it in a context in which the sound makes sense. I do this by looking around me, at the world as it presents itself to me. I am in bed, but it is not my bed. In fact, I am not in a familiar room. There is a mirror and the curtains are strange, and there is the sound. Then I remember: I am in a hotel room. The shrieking sound is the alarm I set, which I found, bizarrely, forming part of the television. I crawl out of bed and fumble with the various buttons until the alarm is turned off, or at least I think it is turned off, only to hear the shrieking sound start up again when I am in the shower. Apparently, I hit the snooze button.

The point of the example, of course, is to demonstrate that the world presents itself, in part, as evidence of past organizations/actions. The fact that it presents such evidence is a function of its having been so organized in the past.

Now the point I want to draw from this is that the past is only part of an overall picture, the other two parts being the present and the future, but it is a part with a specific role. The past is that part of the world that reveals itself as evidence and therefore can yield *knowledge.* Permit me to insist here too, because the idea expressed here contrasts with a view that would want to situate knowledge in the present, in contact with present reality. However, it is more accurate to say that *confirmation* is what takes place in contact with present reality, confirmation of knowledge structured and organized in the past. The night before: oh, there's the alarm clock! Why is it part of the television? The following morning: what is that horrible sound? Oh, it's the alarm clock. Thus our knowledge, gained from consideration of the past, is confirmed, or disconfirmed, in our contact with the world in the present. Indeed, this is precisely how I want to characterize the present's contribution to the overall picture I am attempting to paint: the present describes the line of contact with the reality of the world.

This notion of *contact,* I think, helps us make sense of the strangeness of the present, when you stop and think about it. The present never seems to stand still, never seems simply to be. It is always pointing to the future, as well as perpetually becoming past. Though we are often told to live for "today," for the "now," we can't, because there doesn't seem to be a stable, enduring now we could get a hold of. Are we talking about now, or now? Perhaps now. No, now.

Now! NOW! Always the present yields to the past, but, strangely, by pointing to the future. Having said that, in another sense all we ever really have is the present, in the sense that the past is no longer and the future is not yet.

In the context of the question we are asking, we can see the present as playing a very specific role: it describes our connection or contact with the world as it *presents* itself to us. It presents itself in highly organized ways, thanks to the past, but always through contact, as present. That contact can lead us to question the past, organized world for any number of reasons. What *is* that sound?

The picture we have so far is that the world presents itself to us through organized and structured (via the past) contact (via the present). However, we should recall that our question does not concern merely the world as it presents itself, as though it were presenting itself to no one in particular. If that were the case, then would be no point in saying that it presents itself, would there? The question also concerns the world as it presents itself to *us*, such that we effectively take our bearings within it, move within it, make our way through it. This requires that we think that our structured contact with the world is not a fixed contact but one that admits of *change*. What we know from the past and confirm in present contact does not tell the whole story of our experience of the world. We need to acknowledge that our structured contact with the world does not exhaust the way the world presents itself to us. There is always more to it than our structured contact can handle. Sometimes we ignore that something more, but more often we *anticipate* it. This anticipation of what else there is to the world besides our structured contact with the ways it presents itself to us can be given a simple and straightforward name: it is the future. We don't know the future, for knowledge comes from the past. We don't live in the future, for we exist in the present. We *anticipate* the continued presentation of the world, the future. The future, then, is the world as we do *not* know it and do *not* live it.

Again, we can either ignore the future or anticipate it, but anticipating it rather than ignoring it will better enable us to respond to our initial question. Indeed, it is a concern with the quality of our anticipation that has prompted me to ask and respond to the question posed.

Specifically, I am concerned about two forms of anticipation that have often been formulated, that implicitly respond to our question and that have been influential. However, I believe them to be inadequate to the world as it actually presents itself to us. I believe them to be inadequate because they do not fully appreciate the historicity of the world that they are attempting to elucidate. That is, their anticipation does not adequately appreciate the most important features of our contemporary structured contact with the world as it presents itself to us.

The first form formulates our anticipation in terms that suggest that we have reached some kind of destination, some kind of plateau or even summit, in our journey as human beings. In a word, that, as far as where we are headed is concerned, we have indeed arrived. This is sometimes expressed by saying that we have reached "the end of history." (Although this notion is usually attributed to Hegel, especially as read by Alexandre Kojève, it has been popularized by Francis Fukuyama in his *The End of History and The Last Man*. Hegel will be discussed in the second part of this work, when we turn to the consideration of our world as "multicultural" and constituted through mutual recognition.) What is meant by "the end of history" is not that time has ceased, or that things will forever remain the same, but rather that, as far as our structured contact with the world is concerned, there is nothing left to anticipate or expect to come out of that structured contact that *we do not already anticipate or expect*.

Before dismissing this formulation outright, as many of us may well want to do out of a healthy respect and understanding for the unknowability of the future, we need to consider more carefully what it being said, not because the formulation is true, but because it is more widespread than one might assume. For example, those who defend the basic definition of a liberal democratic regime—minimally, the free election by all adult voters of those who enact the laws that govern and regulate social relations under a broad conception of human rights—as the best possible regime may in fact do so by either assuming or arguing that it is the only regime that can actually anticipate the basic needs of human beings. Of course, we all recognize that any actually existing regime does not actually *meet* those basic human needs and is rightly criticized for failing to do so. However, the point here is not the practical point of actually meeting those needs—after all, one must realistically concede that the logistics involved in meeting the needs of so many people are pretty complicated and a lot can go wrong a lot of the time—but that of being able to *anticipate* them given our structured contact with the world. In other words, on this view, whatever we *should* anticipate as human beings, we already do, and that is because in liberal democratic regimes we recognize the equal dignity of all human beings. Liberal democratic regimes can certainly be *improved* in terms of their actual delivery of programs that intend to respect that equal dignity, and meet the basic needs that such dignity requires and demands. But no other regime has better *identified* that dignity and those needs. This kind of reasoning certainly does, or at least can be seen to, support the view that we have, as human beings, come to the "end of history." We have succeeded in identifying its goal, that of respecting the dignity of *all* human beings and continuing to attempt to provide for their needs. Given that what will happen in the future is anybody's guess (in the long run), that is, given that the point here is not to predict the future but to anticipate it, then one might be excused for thinking that, whatever *actually* happens, it will either bring us closer to *actual* equal respect as we anticipate it or it will encounter all kinds of difficulties, so many in fact that our anticipation may grow more and more pessimistic, raising the possibility that we may lose our grip on our anticipation, "history" may indeed kick in again and we shall struggle again for a true appreciation of what it means to be human. Hopefully, however, conditions will allow us to notice once again that what it means to be human is to have one's basic needs met and one's dignity respected.

Is there anything wrong with this picture? I shall be arguing that there is, not so much with the picture itself, which I think is splendid and inspiring, but with the manner in which it is painted and exhibited. It is a picture that does not take history, considered as a whole, seriously enough. That is, it doesn't sufficiently appreciate how history as a whole needs to be understood as the past, the present, and the future taken together: what I am going to call the past-present-future complex, in order to distinguish the notion of history as a whole from the notion of history as the study of the past. As well, it does not sufficiently appreciate how we in effect situate ourselves within this past-present-future complex. Such an appreciation will require that we develop a more *modally sophisticated* account of how we relate to the past-present-future complex. By "modally sophisticated" I mean an account that takes into consideration the concepts of *possibility*, *necessity*, and *contingency*.

Before we do that, there is another form of anticipation that is becoming more and more prevalent, though it gets expressed differently from both ends of the political spectrum. It holds that, if we maintain the kinds of structured contact with the world that we currently have, then we are headed towards disaster. For some, that means ecological disaster: we are ruining the very conditions that sustain our continued existence by depleting our resources, poisoning our atmosphere, initiating genetic mutations that cannot be controlled, and the result will be the collapse of our interrelated societies (much as described in, for example, Jared Diamond's recent book *Collapse: How Societies Choose to Fail or Succeed*). Others argue that we are headed toward social and political disaster in the shape of conflicts and clashes, if not outright war, again because our current modes of structuring our contact do not adequately sustain the conditions for continued existence, or rather, because the conditions we are speaking of here are explicitly social and political, the conditions for our continued *co*-existence (one thinks here of Samuel P. Huntington's *The Clash of Civilizations and the Remaking of World Order*). These people point to all the unrest we see throughout the world, in the Middle East especially, but also in Africa or East Asia.

This approach is in many ways the mirror image of the "end of history" approach. While those arguing for the "end of history" display a basic optimism in their idea that human beings can look forward, *given present circumstances* (which include the ways in which those present circumstances are ordered and organized), to a future that will not betray their present anticipations, those arguing that the future will involve collapse or conflict are much more pessimistic. Interestingly, however, the pessimists, like the optimists, do *not* think, again given present circumstances, that the future will betray their present anticipations. It is merely the case that they describe that future in more negative terms. They paint a darker picture, as it were, using darker colours and more sombre figures.

While it is neither true nor helpful to think of all the optimists as "progressives" and all the pessimists as "conservatives," there is a sense in which the former emphasize that which, within our present circumstances, allows us to envisage *progress* in the realization of the ideals that can be found within them, while the latter tend to emphasize that which, within our present circumstances, needs to be *conserved* in the face of the destructive forces that threaten them. Both, however—and this is the point I wish to underline—envision their future through their anticipations *from an essentially fixed conception of the present*, as it reads the past and relates to the future. The reason for this, as I shall attempt to show, is that they do not allow their anticipations *to question the structured organization of their (position in the) present*. That is, they both take their present, and the way it is structurally organized in its contact with reality, for granted and as in some way *fixed*, even if, indeed *as*, they think that this present can and, optimistically or pessimistically, *will* lead to that which their anticipations hope for or fear.

What both these positions do, then, is abstract the present, or their present understanding of what that present is, from the actual flow of history. From that abstracted position they project a particular future, ideally conceived. However, as I hope to show in this book, if we are going to try to think about how to respond philosophically to the question of where we are headed, which is largely a question about how the future relates to the present, which itself arises out of the past, then we would do well to put the categories of pessimism and optimism to one side. They only cloud the issue.

Instead, we need to try to develop a more modally sophisticated understanding of our relationship to the way in which our lives unfold within the past-present-future complex. We need to think of the world less as a "thing" that confronts us than as that which permits us to move about, to be oriented, an unfolding as it were. Nothing mysterious is meant by this. You open your eyes and, if there is sufficient light, you begin to see. Yes, you see things, but your seeing them is largely a matter of positioning them with regard to what you are doing. The world is that which allows this positioning to unfold.

We need to think of the world, and of our relating to that world, in *modal* terms, in terms of what it allows, forbids, promises, denies. In logical terms, we want to think of the world in terms of the *possibilities* that it contains, the *necessities* that it displays, the *impossibilities* that delimit it, and the *contingencies* that describe it.

Michel Serres, a French philosopher who worked for a long time at Stanford University, suggests (in his *Hominescence*, p. 191) that we consider these concepts as describing the "modal square" (*le carré des modalités*) that characterizes our existence, the world within which our lives unfold. Rather than think in ontological terms of our *being* in a world, we want to think our existences within this modal square, which Serres describes in the following way (my translation):

> . . . subjected to necessity, gravity, cold, hunger, thirst . . . we choose among and undergo, without cease, a hundred hoped for or projected possibilities, filtered through as many impossibilities, a time, a future, a contingent existence. I might not have so lived, but cannot go back: from the present to the past, contingency turns into necessity, where things will no longer change. I do not know my future, in effect unexpected, upon which I press my hopes and preparations, without being lulled with unrealizable dreams—though, sometimes, by chance, a miracle. . . . From the present to the future, the necessary turns into the possible; filtered by the impossible, it emerges as contingent.

What we want to focus on is the way in which the modal terms—possibility, necessity, and contingency—relate to each other in this unfolding of our lives, and thus help us make sense of that unfolding. I insist on it as an unfolding, each day unfolding over into the next and folding into it elements that we retain from the previous days: that is indeed how we live our lives.

The contingent kicks things off. I might not have existed, but I do. So much for being but how do I exist? By taking advantage of what is possible for me to do, which includes recognizing what is necessary (food, shelter, the fact that I cannot fly unassisted) and what is impossible (to live forever, to run faster than a speeding bullet, never to make a mistake). Note, further, the *direction* that describes how these concepts relate within our lives. Looking back from the present, what was contingent has become necessary, for you cannot change the past. Looking forward from the present, we enact possibilities against a backdrop of impossibilities. The necessities of the past as they enable us to move into the future show themselves to be contingent. *The story begins and ends with the notion that things could have been, or could be, different.* This progressive realization of contingency through necessity is filtered through our enactment of possibilities left open by the impossible.

These are the modal connections that we need to keep in mind as we continue to respond to our question concerning where we are headed in this increasingly multicultural world. How have the necessities of the past produced this contingent world? Which possibilities do its impossibilities allow? How are they to be realized?

The modal square within which we live out our lives needs to be thought within the past-present-future complex. If I say that our knowledge belongs to the past, it is because knowledge deals with the necessities that we come to recognize as structuring our world. We must remember, however, that those necessities are themselves *contingently known* by knowers in contact with a present reality. Any given knower might not have been and the knowledge might be lost. Thus, even the necessities that we know are not given to us once and for all, but rather inscribe themselves within a contingent present, which itself, as contingent, is structurally open to the possibilities of the future.

But, someone might ask at this point, is this focus on the past, the present, *and* the future really necessary? The past is past, it is gone. As for the future, while it is true that it depends to some extent on what we do today, and therefore is legitimately factored into our decision-making, it remains unknowable as such, and therefore our focus should be on the present. My response here is to remind us of the reasonableness of our question: where are we headed? When we attempt to think through the "we," we see how it cannot be isolated from the past-present-future complex. Our sense of "we" arises out of the past and moves forward into the future. In doing so, it determines the shape of our present, the world as it is lived in contact. What our question demands is that we widen the scope of that complex. This involves understanding how our sense of ourselves has arisen out of the past and how it is moving into the future *such that* it shapes our present in the particular ways that it does, enabling us to answer our question.

In response to the objection, our focus *is* on the present. It is just that the present is being understood, not in isolation, but within the context of what I am calling the past-present-future complex (history considered as a whole). The characterization of this complex is constructed by distinguishing the different roles of *knowledge* (the past), *structured contact* (the present), and *anticipation* (the future). A more complex version of our initial question thus becomes: how can what we know of how the past has structured our present, such that we anticipate what we do, help us understand where we are headed?

I suspect that many readers will shortly abandon me if I remain at this level of abstraction. However, what appears to be an abstract discussion is merely a *general* one. The reader can make it more concrete and particular at any time by looking up from the page and considering her surrounding world. It is that world that I am attempting to make sense of, with specific reference to its "increasingly multicultural" character, which means, minimally, that we recognize that referring to who "we" are and where "we" are headed, given "our" past, is a rather complex affair. That is, as soon as one leaves the confines of one's private surroundings as these have been shaped into one's particular place in the world—one's home, office or other personally managed space—one cannot help but acknowledge that the surrounding world is not completely structured around one's familiarities.

Recall the example of the bus ride where different languages are spoken. Indeed, the same point can be made without leaving the confines of one's home. One need only turn on the television and flip through the channels, or spend some time surfing the internet. Much will be familiar and reflective of one's own perspective, but much will also be unfamiliar. Think again here of what news programs deem important enough to bring to your attention. My point is that one's *contact* with the world—the *present* component in the past-present-future complex—is one that is structured in such a way that one's familiarities are increasingly challenged by *other* familiarities, other ways of making sense of the world with which each of us is increasingly called upon to interact and recognize as describing our overall conditions of coexistence. This is the sense I am giving to the "multicultural" in the title of this book: our world is increasingly structured by the contact of different familiarities, different ways of making sense of the world. What such a world of contrasting familiarities demands of us, I shall try to argue, is a renewed attempt to articulate the conditions and possibilities that such a world offers.

This book should be read as a contribution to that rearticulation. What characterizes my particular contribution is that it will appeal to what has traditionally been called "speculative philosophy of history" because I think that it provides a very fruitful approach to answering the nagging question of "where we are headed" and is a way to make fuller sense of the observation that the world is "becoming increasingly multicultural."

PART I
One World

I

Kant and the Cosmopolitan Point of View

The three texts in speculative philosophy of history that are to be examined in this book are all relatively short. The first is by Immanuel Kant and was written in 1784: "Idea for a Universal History from a Cosmopolitan Point of View." It is especially useful for us because it is written in the form of nine theses concerning the very *idea* of thinking of history as a whole, or "Universal History." Given the title that Kant gave to this piece, we should note right away that the attempt to consider the *whole* of history must nevertheless take place from a particular perspective or point of view. None of us is God, and we cannot examine the whole of history from on high, as it were, as a spectacle to be contemplated from a position *outside* history.

For Kant, a position that enables us to consider the whole of history can be found if we adopt a *cosmopolitan* point of view. The idea of cosmopolitanism is quite popular at the present time because it captures the sense we increasingly have of all belonging to one world, despite the diversities that the world exhibits. Kwame Anthony Appiah captures this sense quite well in his book *Cosmopolitanism: Ethics in a World of Strangers* when he identifies (p. xv):

> two strands that intertwine in the notion of cosmopolitanism. One is the idea
> that we have obligations to others, obligations that stretch beyond those to whom
> we are related by the ties of kith and kin, or even the more formal ties of a shared
> citizenship. The other is that we take seriously the value not just of human life but
> of particular human lives, which means taking an interest in the practices and beliefs
> that lend them significance. People are different, the cosmopolitan knows, and there
> is much to learn from our differences.

Such a sense is, of course, accentuated by the fact that all kinds of people travel all over the world, in ways that would have been unimaginable not so long ago. Kant, after all, was writing at the end of the eighteenth century, when travel was not what it is today. (It was even worse than what my grandparents must have experienced when they set out from Quebec and Massachusetts to their homestead in Saskatchewan in the first decades of the twentieth century, which itself was a voyage of epic proportions. In contrast, my son had been to Europe three times before he turned two.)

It is this sense of all of us belonging to one world, which implies that we all have a stake in understanding its development as a whole, that underscores the cosmopolitan point of view. It should be said right away, however, that such a cosmopolitan point of view is difficult to articulate. Think about it: it seeks to comprehend or give some sense to developments that involve the whole world, and to do so from some particular position *within* those developments. By what right can such a point of view claim to be speaking for the development of the whole?

This is a criticism that many people make of cosmopolitanism and what is sometimes characterized as a claim to "world citizenship." Their criticism runs something like this. To be a citizen is to belong to a "city," to a particular locality, not to the world. It involves recognizing those around one, those one interacts with on a daily basis, not everyone or persons halfway across the planet. Yes, I can, today, in a way that I couldn't yesterday, hop on a plane—provided that I have the funds, which is no small consideration—and travel halfway across the planet, but to do so I need a passport attesting to the particular place I occupy within the world. Where do I go when I travel halfway across the planet? Are all neighbourhoods open to me, or do I tend to go where tourists tend to go, stay in hotels that resemble the hotels I am familiar with, eat in restaurants of a kind that I am familiar with from home? Why do I travel halfway across the planet? To meet and discuss things with people who largely already share my concerns and habits, at conferences, for example? What *is* this world of the "world citizen"? Is it *the* world, or the particular world of airport lounges and conference rooms? Is this cosmopolitan "point of view" nothing but the "vantage point of frequent travelers, easily entering and exiting polities and social relations around the world, armed with visa-friendly passports and credit cards" (as Craig Calhoun calls it in his article, "The Class Consciousness of Frequent Travelers")?

Such considerations lead many to abandon the attempt to articulate a cosmopolitan point of view out of a concern for the danger of misrepresenting, distorting, or ignoring other points of view. There is much to be said for such a concern. However, the fact remains that we do share a planet as human beings and that, in a very real sense, we *do* have a point of view on the world as a whole, namely, that it is our world. This raises all kinds of questions whose answers appeal to this sense of belonging to one world. Cosmopolitans insist that we should "think global" (while some insist that at the same time we should "act local"), which means to think about, among other things, the exploitation and distribution of the planet's resources, our modes of consumption and the impact they have on the environment (think, for example, of the greenhouse effect or the various threats that are posed to biodiversity), and questions of international security. Think also about poverty, the causes of warfare in different parts of the world, terrorist acts, literacy, the spread of diseases, natural disasters. Then, of course, there are questions raised by the spread of networks that span the entire globe, whether financial or humanitarian, or the circuits of migration of people, products, drugs and the internet. Can such networks be regulated? If so, by whom, and how?

I do not mean to ask these questions rhetorically. There are very serious efforts to develop a cosmopolitan point of view that responds in a complex and "layered" way to the concerns raised. The work of David Held in this regard is exemplary. While recognizing that we do live "locally," we cannot ignore the fact that what is done locally can have effects far and wide. We should not oversimplify the problem, however, by restricting ourselves to identifying a "local" dimension and a "global" dimension to the world. In his article "Democratic Accountability and Political Effectiveness from a Cosmopolitan Perspective" Held argues for a "cosmopolitan multilateralism" that recognizes, not only that different levels of governance can respond to the different levels of problems, but also (p. 382) that the whole

> must take as its starting point a world of "overlapping communities of fate."
> Recognizing the complex processes of an interconnected world, it ought to view
> certain issues—such as housing, education, and policing—as appropriate for spatially
> delimited political spheres (the city, region or state), while seeing others—such as the
> environment, world health and global economic regulation—as requiring new, more
> extensive institutions to address them.

I think that Held's expression "overlapping communities of fate" nicely captures the sense we have of belonging to one world even while we recognize that the world is composed of very diverse communities. Whatever the diversity of all these communities, we increasingly have the sense that our *fate* is a shared one insofar as we share the same planet. The expression also nicely captures the sense we have that our continued coexistence is moving us in a certain direction.

Thinking about this direction is the traditional concern of the speculative philosophy of history. In fact, speculative philosophy of history, especially as classically formulated, is an attempt to *think* about the sense we have of participating in a wider movement that seems to be directed to some end. It is speculative because there is no claim to *know* the end to which we are moving. It is philosophical because it seeks to interrogate that movement, and not merely hand it over to something like "fate," as more traditionally conceived. It speaks of history because it seeks to situate that movement within an intelligible framework, the past-present-future complex, that is, history considered as a whole.

For Kant, what does it mean to consider "history as a whole"? It means, first, that one is trying to understand it as more than the desolate spectacle it otherwise reveals itself to be. When Kant, who participated in the Enlightenment's celebration of human beings' capacity to understand the world by the use of their rational faculties, contemplates the course of world history, he is frankly puzzled. He writes in "Idea for a Universal History from a Cosmopolitan Point of View" (p. 12):

> One cannot suppress a certain indignation when one sees men's actions on the great world-stage and finds, beside the wisdom that appears here and there among individuals, everything in the large woven together from folly, childish vanity, even from childish malice and destructiveness. In the end, one does not know what to think of the human race, so conceited in its gifts.

Kant does not rest content with this puzzlement. On the contrary—and this perhaps defines the philosopher better than anything—such puzzlement spurs him on to thought. He continues:

> Since the philosopher cannot presuppose any [conscious] individual purpose among men in their great drama, there is no other expedient for him except to try to see if he can discover a natural purpose in this idiotic course of things human. In keeping with this purpose, it might be possible to have a history with a definite natural plan for creatures who have no plan of their own.

The point that needs to be emphasized here from the beginning is the idea that the rationality of the historical process is sought, not so much *despite* its apparent senselessness, its wars and other destructive conflicts, but precisely *because of* that apparent senselessness. That senselessness is *apparent*, which does not mean here that it is not *real*, literally because that is what "appears" to the observer. What happens to the appearance, however, when one attempts to *think* it? Well, insofar as one attempts to *think* the apparent senselessness, one *brings* (attempts to bring) sense to those appearances. This is what thinking about the historical process brings to it, or out of it: the sense that it contains, if any. Now, given that the attempt to think the sense of history itself belongs to history—we do not stand outside history when we try to make sense of it—then there is hope and reason to think that the attempt will be rewarded, if only one knows where to look.

Kant's idea was to look to Nature, because scientific investigation had shown that Nature could yield rational structures that were not immediately apparent. Perhaps History, too, when properly investigated, would yield such rational structures. Kant's basic idea here was that the regularities that Nature manifests when investigated properly might also manifest themselves in History. History distinguishes itself from Nature, according to Kant, as the stage upon which human *willing* manifests itself, that is, History describes human *actions*, those things that human beings undertake willingly and willfully, and which, if observed in any particular instance, can appear quite chaotic and arbitrary. (How many times have you asked yourself: Why in the world did X do that? X, of course, can mean you yourself.) Kant wants to entertain the speculative possibility ("Idea . . .," p. 11) that:

> if we attend to the play of freedom of the human will in the large, we may be able to discern a regular movement in it, and that what seems complex and chaotic in the single individual may be seen from the standpoint of the human race as a whole to be a steady and progressive though slow evolution of its original endowment.

Thus, for Kant, the cosmopolitan point of view is the point of view or "standpoint" of the whole human race. What do things look like from that perspective? How might we articulate that perspective? Kant proposes nine speculative "theses" that seek to grasp the historical process as a whole, which Kant calls "Universal History." There are all kinds of reasons for rejecting any individual thesis, as will quickly become evident. However, to reject them too quickly would be to fail to engage with their speculative character. What I am interested in is the light they throw on the question of where we are headed, given the increasingly multicultural character of the world considered as a whole.

The first thesis Kant states is that: "All natural capacities of a creature are destined to evolve completely to their natural end." (Note that Kant was writing before the elaboration and general acceptance of the theory of evolution.) This is a teleological claim. It attempts to make sense of its object by referring to the presumed end to which it is directed, which is another way of saying that any particular object is related to other objects as parts within a *whole*. Teleology is an important mode of thinking for articulating the orientation of things within the whole. The point here, then, is that in referring to *capacities*—abilities to do something or other—we implicitly include a reference to the ends or goals that inhere in the doing of this or that. Given this teleological whole, the idea of speculating about their evolution in terms of an ultimate completion does not seem to be unreasonable. For example, you may have an ear for music, which is a particular capacity. Your parents or teachers notice this and encourage you to learn how to play an instrument, which itself is an elaborate development of the human capacity to hear and make music. Depending on your particular ability and the encouragement you receive, in material terms especially, your "ear for music" will develop in a specific direction, or many different directions, but always with reference to an overall context of musical development. "Nature," for Kant, simply means the overall context for the development of *all* capacities.

Now, pretty clearly, not all human capacities can be developed within the lifespan and the range of particular endowments of a single individual. Hence, Kant's second thesis: "In man (as the only rational creature on Earth) those natural capacities which are directed to the use of reason are to be fully developed only in the race, not in the individual." This is fairly straightforward and obvious. However, the point I would like to draw attention to is how "Nature" in the statement of this thesis is at the same time the introduction of *history*, understood as the *development over time of human capacities*, a connected and ongoing story of achievement, the whole of which speculative philosophy of history tries to make sense. As Kant goes on to remark:

> a single man would have to live excessively long in order to learn to make full use of all his natural capacities. Since Nature has set only a short period for his life, she needs a perhaps unreckonable series of generations, each of which passes its own enlightenment to its successors in order finally to bring the seeds of enlightenment to that degree of development in our race which is completely suitable to Nature's purpose.

Kant, importantly, adds:

> This point of time must be, at least as an ideal, the goal of man's efforts, for otherwise his natural capacities would have to be counted as for the most part vain and aimless.

Here we see the prime motivation of speculative thinking: it attempts to *think* the whole in order to provide some account of the *direction* our various efforts may be taking. If we do not try to think the whole within which we evolve as rational human beings, our lives will be merely aimless existences of more or less animated bodies governed by basic satisfactions. The concern is that our capacities and abilities will atrophy if not given the direction and scope that a speculative grasp of a developing whole is meant to provide.

Now, before delving deeper into this basic claim for the importance of speculative philosophy of history, I would like to relate these matters once again to the context of our question of where we are headed, but now with emphasis on the observation I also identified concerning how our world is becoming increasingly multicultural. Part of what this observation affirms is that we recognize in the world many different ways of life. This, of course, has always been the case. An "increasingly multicultural" world, however, is one where these different ways of life are increasingly in contact with one another, and therefore are called upon to establish and regulate relations with one another.

This observation is not merely an empirical one. It also implies that the variety of ways of life encountered in the world, because of their increasing contact, raises problems and questions that need to be resolved. For some, such as Will Kymlicka, the observation leads to discussions concerning the "integration" of these various cultures or ways of life within a coherent and stable whole that respects the differences that these ways of life display. For others, such as Samuel P. Huntington, it raises the question of establishing and maintaining forms of "segregation," again in the name of coherence and stability.

The question that interests me is the traditional philosophical one about whether or not there is a truly human way of life to which all human beings should aspire. The general consensus of those who make the observation that the world is becoming increasingly multicultural is surely that there is not such a way of life. The view that there is, or should be, a conception of a *truly* human way of life to which all human beings should aspire is called by some theorists, such as Bhikhu Parekh, "moral monism," in contrast to "moral pluralism," which recognizes that truly human lives can be lived in a variety of ways. Parekh believes that such an idea is "logically incoherent." Such an idea, he says in his *Rethinking Multiculturalism* (p. 48):

> rests on the naïve assumption that valuable human capacities, desires, virtues and dispositions form a harmonious whole and can be combined without loss. Human capacities conflict for at least three reasons, namely intrinsically and because of the limitations of the human condition and the constraints of social life: the first, because they often call for different, even contradictory skills, attitudes and dispositions, and the development of some of them renders that of others difficult if not impossible; the second, because human energies, motivations, and resources are necessarily limited, and one can cultivate only some of the valuable human capacities; and the third, because every social order has a specific structure with its inescapable tendency to develop some capacities rather than others and allow only certain ways of combining them. Since human capacities conflict, the good they are capable of realizing also conflicts. Like human capacities, values and virtues too conflict. Justice and mercy, respect and pity, equality and excellence, love and impartiality, moral duties to humankind and to one's kith and kin often point in different directions, and are not easily reconciled. In short, every way of life, however good it might be,

entails a loss. And since it is difficult to say which of these values are higher, both in the abstract and in specific contexts, the loss involved cannot be measured and compared, rendering unintelligible the idea of a particular way of life as representing the highest good.

Much of what Parekh says here certainly rings true, especially within the context of an increasingly multicultural world. What happens, however, if we place Parekh's considerations within the context of the speculative philosophy of history, with particular reference to Kant's claim that the unfolding of history needs to be understood as the full and complete development of human capacities?

The first thing to note is that Parekh is quite right to remind us that, when we discuss different ways of life, we are not talking about harmonious wholes that unfold without conflict and contestation, even if, to be considered as particular ways of life, they must display *some* cohesion and coherence to those who adopt and adapt those ways. Otherwise we would have no reason to identify them as particular *ways* of life. It is also good to remind ourselves that what makes a particular way of life *particular* is that it develops certain features or possibilities available to human beings, without exhausting all of them. This corresponds to the third point raised by Parekh, namely, that "every social order has a specific structure with its inescapable tendency to develop some capacities rather than others and allow only certain ways of combining them."

Right off, one might question the claim that such tendencies are "inescapable." If by that Parekh means that the development of those particular capacities is what *defines* a particular way of life, describing one of its salient features as a particular way of life, then it makes sense to say that such tendencies can be considered "inescapable," within that particular way of life. However, I suspect that Parekh means "inescapable" in a stronger, more specific sense: namely, that one cannot get away from the development of those capacities, that, in a real sense, one is trapped in them insofar as one participates in that way of life. An escape from them can be accomplished only by abandoning that way of life or, perhaps more accurately, by excluding oneself from it.

Think about the capacity to read, for example. This is something that many cultures insist on and seek to develop in everyone who "belongs" to a culture. It is a particular capacity, insofar as human beings can and do live out their lives without developing it, but it is one that is "inescapable" in many cultures, insofar as its development is considered a requirement for full participation in that particular way of life. People who fail to develop that capacity in the required way are subject to remedial strategies meant to correct that failure. Some people who fail to develop that capacity may succeed in concealing the fact by "faking" it. However, this only underlines the "inescapability" of the development of that capacity within that particular way of life. Such an example underscores Parekh's additional claim that any particular way of life, simply because it is particular, "entails a loss." That is, because certain capacities are developed, and not others, then any given way of life will foreclose the development of other capacities that, considered from the perspective of the development of *all* human capacities (which we do not have to presume to be able to identify), represents a "loss."

Again, this all sounds very reasonable, especially given our increasingly "multicultural" recognition and awareness of different ways of life. Not so long ago, the awareness of different ways of life did not provoke such attitudes of tolerant resignation, but instead fuelled missionary zeal. However, even though Parekh seems to be arguing against moral monism, which insists on only one *truly* human way of life, it seems to me that the language Parekh is using here in an important sense *presupposes* something very like the monism he wishes to combat. Specifically, why should we consider the fact that any given way of life does not develop *all* human capacities as indicative of a loss? A loss of what? Presumably of a way of life that, even if only ideally, *did* develop all human capacities. But that would be to subscribe to the view that we can imagine, or speculate about, a single way of life that we would be tempted to call a truly human life. Of course, one might want to point out here that there are many human capacities that are less than laudable, such as the capacity to kill each other, or the capacity of the strong to dominate the weak, and we might insist on *not* developing them. The lack of development of these particular capacities would not be seen as a "loss" either. Note, too, that Parekh himself, in the paragraph quoted above, ends up saying that "the loss involved cannot be measured and compared." If that is the case, then one might be led to wonder why the notion of loss is invoked at all. There seems to be no potential for gain or loss, only different particular ways of life and their respective development of particular capacities. Yet Parekh does invoke it in order to criticize moral monism, which, I remind the reader, means a "naïve" assumption of harmoniousness.

Now, we might ask ourselves why the assumption of "harmoniousness," as an ideal to be ultimately achieved by human beings—for some, in this world, for others, in the next—should be considered "naïve." I am always suspicious of charges of naïveté. They tend to say more about the accuser than they do about the accused, and what they say is that the accuser sees himself as disabused and hard-headed about reality, and therefore considers his outlook to be superior to the woolly and wishful thinking of the naïf. However true this may be in any particular instance—for all of us are subject to woolly and wishful thinking on occasion—contact with reality is not a function of hard-headedness. Technically, contact with reality is a function of being *alive*, although of course the quality of that contact varies considerably: it can be sharp or dim, concentrated or listless, and so on. Therefore the naïf is as much in contact with reality as the disabused critic is, although according to the latter he may be in contact with it in a childish way.

Does this mean that when Parekh says that it is naïve to assume that "valuable human capacities, desires, virtues and dispositions form a harmonious whole and can be combined without loss," he is saying that thinking this is somehow childish? Probably. Indeed, one can imagine a child, or rather a young person, thinking about the *possibility* of living a life that will combine his or her various capacities and desires, as well as particular virtues and dispositions, in such a way as to form "a harmonious whole." One can even imagine such a young person imagining that his or her life, combined with the lives of others, may also yield such a "a harmonious whole," if only the conditions are somehow right.

Now, to *assume* that all human capacities taken together—those we are familiar with, those we can imagine and, perhaps, those we cannot—form a harmonious whole is no doubt a mistake, if by "assume" here one means "take as true without regard for evidence." However, I doubt that the young person in such a case is doing that. The harmonious whole that he or she aspires to is not treated as already existing, but as a *possibility*, stemming from the fact that the capacities in question are human and the young person sees him or herself as human.

One sees here more clearly why the charge of "naïveté" gets raised. This young person is inexperienced and does not (yet) know what the world does to such aspirations. Soon enough, he or she will come to realize the kinds of things that Parekh outlines: the constraints imposed on the development of our capacities, their tendency to conflict, as well as their inherent limitations, all precluding any possibility of their being combined into a harmonious whole. A more extended experience of the world will teach all this to the young person as he or she grows older. The person was naïve to think this in the first place, but perhaps understandably so. To continue to think it as one grows older, however, is to be naïve in a less acceptable way.

I am prepared to concede for the sake of the argument, and pending future discoveries about ways of living unheard of today, that the harmonious whole aspired to by such young persons, as well as by some not so young persons, has so far and systematically not materialized in the different ways of life that human beings have devised. Yet I still think that Parekh is making a mistake in rejecting this possibility *in principle*. This seems to me to make the faulty assumption that the future will necessarily resemble the past. If one places the harmonious whole aspired to within the modal square within which our lives unfold, then its *possibility* takes on a different meaning. Its *possibility* contrasts with the various impossibilities of a given social order that are a function of the necessities that have structured its past. *These* are the constraints that Parekh mentions. Rather than tie them too quickly to something called the "human condition," one should consider them within the context of the past-present-future complex, or history considered as a whole. This means taking seriously the distinct roles that the past, the present, and the future play in our thinking about this developing whole.

Of course, insofar as the future will carry on the knowledge we currently have, then in that sense the future will indeed resemble the past, as per our definitions. However, as we have seen, the future is a question of our *anticipations* given the way the world presents itself to us, which includes that which we claim to be knowledgeable about, that is, the past. Parekh may have excluded from his own anticipations the possibility of a harmonious whole materializing out of our various human capacities, for the reasons he gives, but I believe that he does so hastily and out of a misconception of the role that anticipations (the future) can and should play in our attempts to make sense of the world as it presents itself to us.

Although our anticipations arise out of our knowledge of the world (the past) through continued contact with it (the present), they should not be confused with, or reduced to, that knowledge. All we should be really claiming as knowledge is that the world has not, in the past, exhibited our various capacities as forming a harmonious whole. On the contrary, knowledge of the (past) world demonstrates much more forcefully the conflict-ridden ways that our capacities have developed. Far be it from me to dismiss such knowledge. However, in *my* contact with the (present) world, perhaps because I teach young people, this knowledge includes the expression of aspirations that include reference to the harmonious whole eschewed by Parekh. Such aspirations are perhaps relatively uninformed, because lacking in knowledge, but that does not affect them *as aspirations* within a particular contact with the (present) world. This demonstrates to me, *contra* Parekh, that the aspiration to a harmonious whole, far from being a naïve assumption, is in fact a privileged locus for trying to understand what role the future (what we anticipate) plays in the past-present-future complex.

My guess is that the rejection of any conception that would have the past-present-future complex comprise a harmonious whole, a rejection that Parekh shares with a wide spectrum of his contemporaries, is more a rejection of the idea of "wholeness" than it is of the idea of "harmoniousness". There is an insistence in contemporary thinking on leaving things open, not closing them up into any overall scheme of things. However, this insistence is too often not sufficiently thought through and, indeed, is often contradicted in practice. Parekh is a case in point. He treats our various human capacities as impossible to combine into a harmonious whole and as always involving, in any particular combination, a *loss*. In doing so he at once rejects *and* accepts the idea of a harmonious whole. He rejects the possibility of its actualization, but then accepts its conceptualization in order to evaluate the way in which any actual combination fails to match up to it (by characterizing it as involving a loss). Why should any *particular* combination of actually developing human capacities, because they do not *exhaust* all human capacities, be characterized as involving some kind of loss? Such a characterization depends, it seems to me, on an implicit conception of a non-particular (universal) combination of all human capacities that we never, in our particular attempts to combine our capacities, actually achieve—or to be precise, that we have never been able to achieve *in the past*.

However, we should not restrict ourselves to consideration of the past. Rather, like Kant, we should consider the past, the present, and the future as a whole, and we should think about how different ways of life develop within the modal square. Recall that, if I say that our knowledge belongs to the past, it is because knowledge deals with the necessities we come to recognize as structuring our world. Yet we must remember that those necessities are themselves *contingently known* by knowers in contact with a present reality, for any given knower might not have been and the knowledge might be lost. Thus, even the necessities that we know are not given to us once and for all, but rather are inscribed within a contingent present, which itself, as contingent, is structurally open to the possibilities of the future.

This, I believe, is what the young person senses when he or she considers the possibility of a future open to the harmonious development of his or her capacities. Because the necessities he or she knows have not been translated into practical *im*possibilities, he or she remains open to possibility in an anticipatory way foreclosed by those who project known necessities onto the future. The proper way to integrate known necessities into one's projections is to recognize that possibilities actually arise against the backdrop of impossibilities, which themselves are contingently encountered.

If we bring this back to the development of human capacities, one may already *know* that the development of *all* of one's capacities is a practical impossibility. However, against the backdrop of that practical impossibility, the possibility nevertheless remains that one might *combine* the development of one's capacities in such a way that they produce a harmonious whole. It may very well be the case that such efforts fail, for any number of reasons, including the ones identified by Parekh: inherent limitations, conflicts that arise out of constraints encountered, and so on. Yet such failures remain *contingencies*, not necessities. On the contrary, the anticipation that fuels the effort helps define the nature of the continuing possibility against the backdrop of contingently encountered impossibilities.

Another way of putting this is that we should not be too quick to convert our sense of possibilities into one of probabilities. The calculation of probabilities takes as fixed the framework within which predictions are made. The anticipation of possibilities opens up that framework by recognizing the unknowability of the future and the contingency of the present. The point is not to devise predictions that will then be tested by actual experience, but to *anticipate* one's experience within that open future, given what one knows, certainly, but recognizing the limits of that knowledge, given its place within the modal square and the past-present-future complex.

This is where the notion of a harmonious whole becomes interesting. If we focus on the "harmony" rather than the "whole"—given that the "whole," because it is being described as a past-present-future complex, is open by definition—then the anticipation is one of a certain contingent co-presence of elements. Think of music, the harmony achieved by an orchestra as it gathers around a particular score and focuses on the conductor's baton. The harmony is an achievement that is sustained in time through individual particular efforts. Compare that achieved "harmonious whole" that is the performance with the pre-performance disharmony of the orchestra tuning its various instruments. That disharmony actually expresses in an anticipatory fashion the harmonious whole that is being sought. Of course, the harmonious whole actually achieved in the performance differs from other performances, those of this particular orchestra and those of other orchestras performing this or some other work, just as such orchestral performances differ from other musical performances. Think of a smoky jazz club where the "harmonious whole" includes, during the performance as opposed to at its end, visceral exclamations of admiration from the audience. Not all performances achieve the kind of "harmonious whole" anticipated, yet the anticipation plays a structural role in the constitution of that whole. If a particular musician isn't "into it," his or her particular anticipation is lacking and the performance suffers.

What is interesting about this example is that it shows how the "harmonious whole" to which the hard-headed refuse to grant actuality is misconceived if it is thought outside of the effort to anticipate it. Indeed, it is precisely within such anticipations that the whole, conceived as harmonious or otherwise, truly finds its place. In other words, the whole is not something that we are doomed to fail to achieve, it is the speculative end of our anticipatory efforts. Our young person, who is only discovering what his true capacities are through a not-yet-discouraged knowledge of what is (im)possible—that is, what possibilities are delimited by contingent constraints—anticipates a life whose speculative end is the full and free development of those capacities in concert with others. He or she knows that such an end is speculative, but that is precisely what fuels and shapes his or her desire.

Now, if we return to Kant, he reminds us (young at heart!) that such full and free development takes *time*, a time longer than any contingently given human life span. The "whole" of the world as it presents itself to us and as we orient ourselves within it, developing the capacities that we are and have, is only "speculatively" present as an unfolding, which Kant calls "Universal History." It is this "Universal History" that provides the ultimate context for the full development of human capacities as these are found in each of us, the ultimate context as seen from the "cosmopolitan point of view." Contemporary attempts to reinvigorate this "cosmopolitan point of view," by insisting on a "global view" or a "global perspective," correctly assume that a view of the whole is the ultimate context for making sense of human development, but they do not sufficiently appreciate the historical dimension of this ultimate context, the simple fact that it *unfolds* in and through time. Indeed, we shall see in a moment that even Kant does not sufficiently appreciate this.

Now, it is important to understand that, when I say that the ultimate context within which human capacities "unfold" (develop) is *historical* time, I am not saying that this is a process that somehow happens automatically. One need only think of one's own capacities as one has learned to identify them, those particular things that one happens to be good at, one's particular talents and abilities, those that others have noticed and encouraged, or at least pointed out. It is quite true that one "discovers" them within oneself, with the help of others. Such capacities are in some sense there already—a musical ear, the ability to run long distances, the ability to draw. However, their *development* requires not only one's own concerted effort, but also a larger social context that allows and provides for that effort. (Howard Gardner calls such abilities "intelligences" and, in his *Frames of Mind: The Theory of Multiple Intelligences*, provides a good discussion of how such intelligences are connected both to the structures of the brain and to the wider social context.)

I am saying nothing new or original here, but I am insisting that such a context and the efforts that are structured by it need to be framed by speculative considerations that involve what Kant calls "Universal History." In other words, our familiar social contexts are insufficient to comprehend fully what is at stake in our own efforts to develop our capacities and to live full human lives. We should not be too quick to reject posing the question, "What is a full human life?" However, in order to respond to it we need to turn to a consideration of "Universal History."

Only *Universal* History can provide the context for the *full* development of human life. Why? Because of the peculiar nature of human life. As Kant says in his third thesis:

MULTICULTURAL DYNAMICS AND THE ENDS OF HISTORY

Nature has willed that man should, by himself, produce everything that goes beyond the mechanical ordering of his animal existence, and that he should partake of no other happiness or perfection than that which he himself, independently of instinct, has created by his own reason.

A full human life is a life whose happiness and perfection is a result of the creative efforts of human reason, and not the mere satisfactions of animal existence. Again, nothing new or original is being said here. However, what I would like to stress is the way in which what Kant calls happiness and perfection are the result of what I am calling the "creative efforts" of *reason*. The point is that "reason" is not something we each possess individually and, as it were, naturally. It is constructed out of the concerted effort of human beings to live together in a way that points them towards their happiness and perfection *as human beings*. Again, typically *human* existence is not the expression of animal satisfactions guided by instinct. It is the contextual development of particular capacities. That contextual development needs to be understood not merely *socially* but *historically*, as involving reference to the past-present-future complex. That is, emphasis needs to be put on the historical context of the particular nature of human sociability. It is within this *historical* context that one can discern and understand the distinctive characteristic of human beings, namely, that their lives are constructed developmentally through the extension of their *reasoning and reasoned* capacities. At least, this is the basic claim of speculative philosophy of history.

We are apt to forget or overlook the specifically historical dimension of our human world. While everyone is prepared to recognize that human beings do not live through instinct, as other animals do, not everyone adequately recognizes the specifically historical dimension of our patterns of sociability, the way in which they are dependent on particular forms of historically motivated development. To illustrate this dependence on specifically *historical* context, as opposed to strictly *social* context, I would like to make use of a "disquieting suggestion" articulated by the philosopher Alasdair MacIntyre in his book *After Virtue: A Study in Moral Theory* (p. 1):

> Imagine that the natural sciences were to suffer the effects of a catastrophe. A
> series of environmental disasters are blamed by the general public on the scientists.
> Widespread riots occur, laboratories are burnt down, physicists are lynched, books
> and instruments are destroyed. Finally a Know-Nothing political movement takes
> power, and successfully abolishes science teaching in schools and universities,
> imprisoning and executing the remaining scientists. Later still there is a reaction
> against this destructive movement and enlightened people seek to revive science,
> although they have largely forgotten what it was. But all that they possess are

fragments: a knowledge of experiments detached from any knowledge of the theoretical context which gave them significance; parts of theories unrelated either to the other bits and pieces of theory which they possess or to experiment; instruments whose use has been forgotten; half-chapters from books, single pages from articles, not always fully legible because torn and charred. Nonetheless, all these fragments are re-embodied in a set of practices which go under the revived names of physics, chemistry, and biology. Adults argue with each other about the respective merits of relativity theory, evolutionary theory, and phlogiston theory, although they possess only a very partial knowledge of each. Children learn by heart the surviving portions of the periodic table and recite as incantations some of the theorems of Euclid. Nobody, or almost nobody, realizes that what they are doing is not natural science in any proper sense at all. For everything that they do and say conforms to certain canons of consistency and coherence, and those contexts which would be needed to make sense of what they are doing have been lost, perhaps irretrievably.

MacIntyre's point in describing this imaginary possible world is to suggest that the state of *moral* theory is in something like the state of the natural sciences in this imaginary world, that is, it is composed of fragments of a tradition that was once coherent, but has been largely destroyed. What we call moral theory today, according to MacIntyre, no longer makes sense, precisely because the contexts within which it did make sense no longer structure human lives, *and we do not even know it*, given that we go on talking about morality as though it still did make sense. Without going into the details of his argument, which is not my concern here, the reason why MacIntyre thinks that moral reasoning no longer makes sense in our real world is that we have no way of resolving moral issues in a way all can agree on, and yet we continue to argue about moral issues, which implies that we think that resolution of such matters is important and relevant.

What I would like to draw from MacIntyre's imaginary world is the way that it graphically illustrates the idea that it is not sociability on its own that provides for the truthfulness of our experience, and yet it is only through sociability that truthfulness is made possible. The natural sciences were destroyed in MacIntyre's imaginary world by human beings who knew what they were doing. They destroyed the conditions under which the natural sciences were conducted, the material and *practical* conditions that gave birth to and sustained the activities of the natural sciences. By killing or imprisoning the scientists, destroying their laboratories and burning their books, and abolishing the contexts within which what natural scientists do was taught to future natural scientists, they effectively wiped out natural science, which we can now see as less a *body* of knowledge than an *embodied* form of knowing. Those later generations that sought to revive the natural sciences could not do so, because they were effectively dead.

The animating spirit that drove the natural sciences forward had been effectively destroyed. This, of course, does not mean that in MacIntyre's imaginary world nothing *like* the natural sciences could be constituted in the activities of human beings as they continued to try to make sense of their world, but it would not arise out of the attempted piecing together of the bits that remain into the body of knowledge that once was. That body would remain a cadaver. Better, perhaps, to bury it and turn one's attention to the world as it presents itself, which, as we have seen, includes knowledge that needs to be confirmed within the present contact with a reality experienced (in modal terms) as the realm of possibility filtered through impossibilities.

It is this *embodied form of knowing*, this dynamic principle of achieved truthfulness through various coordinated activities and practices, that animates our sense of being in a world open to us, a sense encapsulated in the term "reason" as used by Kant and, even more so, by Hegel (as we shall see in the next Part of this book). For Kant, the world—that is, the world as experienced by human beings as something other than "the mechanical ordering of animal existence" —is that which is created through our reasoning efforts. This is the world of *history*, that is, it is not only a *social* world, but a world that is *oriented towards a particular developmental end*. This particular developmental end is what speculative philosophy of history calls the telos of history.

Kant gives an exceptionally clear definition of the telos of history in the eighth thesis of his "Idea of a Universal History from a Cosmopolitan Point of View":

> The history of mankind can be seen, in the large, as the realization of Nature's secret plan to bring forth a perfectly constituted state as the only condition in which the capacities of mankind can be fully developed, and also bring forth that external relation among states which is perfectly adequate to this end.

Speculative philosophy of history concerns itself not only with the telos of history but also with what we are calling its *dynamics*, that which drives the historical process considered as a whole. Indeed, it is the combination of these two components, the *telos* of history with the *dynamics* of history, that not only defines speculative philosophy of history (for our purposes), but allows us to evaluate the relative strengths and weaknesses of particular attempts at formulating speculative philosophies of history. What we are looking for in speculative philosophies of history is a way of better making sense of our world both in terms of its overall direction (its telos) and in terms of the forces that animate it (its dynamics). A speculative philosophy of history should be evaluated in terms of the ways in which it allows us to see how the overall direction that history is taking is *connected* to the dynamic forces that animate history. A successful speculative philosophy of history is one that adequately articulates, in the sense of "linking up" or "connecting," the telos and the dynamics of history.

The questions we need to ask, then, are the following. How does the telos link to the dynamics of history? Are they internally or externally related? That is, does the telos arise out of the dynamics of history, or is the telos something that governs or directs the historical process from some point outside it? One way to think about the significance of these questions is to ask how we are to conceive of the relation of the "real" and the "ideal." That is, how does the real world relate to the ideals that we espouse? Do our ideals govern or direct our dealings in the real world? Are they illusions tossed out by what happens in the real world? If so, why toss out "ideals"? Are ideals generated in and out of our attempts to grapple with the real world? How "real" is the real world if there are no "ideals" to compare it to?

All these questions are stated in a general way but are nevertheless understandable. The particular way in which speculative philosophy of history deals with them is to consider them in terms of the relation between the telos (the ideal) and the dynamics (the real), as these manifest themselves in our attempts to make sense of the historical process considered as a whole. How, then, does Kant fare in this regard? This is what we shall examine in the next chapter.

2

Real Universality as a Challenge to the Cosmopolitan Ideal

We now turn to an evaluation of Kant's speculative effort. As we have said, he has provided an extremely powerful expression of the telos of history. We shall call that expression, as stated in the eighth thesis of his "Idea of a Universal History from a Cosmopolitan Point of View," the "Cosmopolitan Ideal." Its strength, in my view, is that it recognizes and articulates the *historical,* unfolding context of the *full* development of human capacities. Indeed, that it is the point of suggesting this "Idea of a Universal History," because it is only within such a speculative context that the realization of those capacities that we recognize ourselves as possessing can be given their fullest sense.

The weakness of Kant's account, however, lies in the way in which he articulates this Cosmopolitan Ideal with his understanding of the speculative dynamics of history. As it turns out, Kant is not overly impressed with what goes on in a history that can so often be so destructive of human life, "an idiotic course" that, on the face of it, makes little sense. Indeed, as we shall see, even if Kant seems to be engaged in articulating a speculative philosophy of *history,* he is much less concerned with the historical process itself than he is with the *rationality* or the exercise of *reason* that it nevertheless permits, despite appearances to the contrary. It is this commitment to expressions of reason and rationality that underlies his particular reference to the historical process as a whole as revealing a "secret plan of Nature," Nature (with a capital N) meaning for Kant the lawful regularities that human intelligence can grasp. Through his idea that the intelligibility of the historical process as a whole should be grasped as revealing a "secret plan of Nature," Kant actually betrays, if not disdain for, then despair at, what actually goes on "in history," which, if human beings did not also show themselves capable of rational thought, could only be characterized as "this idiotic course of things human." A consequence of this is that Kant's speculative effort does not sufficiently consider how the attempt to articulate the telos of history combines with an understanding of the dynamics of history, of what moves history towards this end.

What is Kant's understanding of the dynamics of history? Kant restricts his consideration to the articulation of the dynamics of *social life* as such, and he appeals to an abstract notion of conflict and antagonism to which he gives the memorable title of "unsocial sociability." His basic idea is that the capacities of human beings develop, and thus serve social life, through the conflicts that otherwise characterize social life. His fourth thesis states:

> The means employed by Nature to bring about the development of all the capacities of men is their antagonism in society, so far as this is, in the end, the cause of lawful order among men.

Thus, for Kant, the motor or the dynamics of social life may be discerned within the dispositions of Nature. History *per se* is merely the stage upon which Nature, through human interaction, acts out its "plan," the rational development of human capacities.

Kant then expands upon the fourth thesis and allows himself to write, with a certain flourish:

> Thanks be to Nature, then, for the incompatibility, for heartless competitive vanity, for the insatiable desire to possess and to rule! Without them, all the excellent natural capacities of humanity would forever sleep, undeveloped. Man wishes concord; but Nature knows better what is good for the race; she wills discord. He wishes to live comfortably and pleasantly; Nature wishes that he be plunged from sloth and passive contentment into labour and trouble, in order that he may find means of extricating himself from them The natural urges to this, the sources of unsociableness and mutual opposition from which so many evils arise, drive men to new exertions of their forces and thus to the manifold development of their capacities.

Thus, in Kant's speculative account, it is an abstract "unsociableness" that drives social life forward towards its end. I say "abstract" because this unsociableness does not *arise* out of social life, but is always already there within social life, as though it were *put there* by Nature as part of its plan for the full development of human capacities. At least, this is the speculative response proposed by Kant, in order to make sense both of the dismal spectacle of human conflict, and of the gains in rational understanding of nature and the idea of lawfulness itself that consideration of history as a whole reveals to him.

Now, it is important to note that, in attributing the realization of the telos of history to a *natural* process (unsocial sociability), Kant is *not* saying that this is something that just happens on its own, without the concerted and intelligent effort of human beings. We must remember the point and function of speculative philosophizing. It is to give us some sense of the whole so that we may direct our efforts to more effect. As Kant states in the ninth and final thesis:

> A philosophical attempt to work out a universal history according to a natural plan directed to achieving the civic union of the human race must be regarded as possible and, indeed, as contributing to this end of Nature.

Indeed, as a *possibility*, its articulation is a cogent, even inspiring response to the question of where we are headed. The problem with this way of articulating the possibility with the telos meant to direct it is that the conception of the dynamics that are to get us there is insufficiently worked out. To put it another way, the problem with Kant's approach is that the dynamic principle does not match the teleological principle.

It is important to understand that from Kant's perspective this is not really a problem, because he is not really concerned with attempting to articulate a telos that is to be realized *in* history. Indeed, Kant is not especially concerned with history. He is concerned with rationality. The principal purpose, perhaps the sole purpose, of articulating a telos and engaging in speculative philosophy of history is to safeguard and to promote the use of reason and rationality, and the appeal to lawfulness that is the ground of that reason and rationality, when thinking about human affairs, even if that is not always easy given the dismal spectacle of our history. The "secret plan of Nature" that Kant proposes as the heart of the historical process, and which is meant to structure it as a whole, is meant to encourage us in the use of our rational faculties and to guard against giving in to despair. The telos it articulates is meant to serve asymptotically as a goal that we forever seek to approach, knowing full well that we shall never achieve it. It proposes a regulative ideal that is meant to guide our rational appreciation and evaluation of our combined efforts.

The problem with this approach, however, is that the telos espoused is not adequately articulated with, or grounded in, the dynamics that are meant to bring that telos about. It appears that our rational faculties cannot wield sufficient power to order conflict in the way that the telos suggests.

Kant was certainly aware of this. In his fifth thesis he states:

> The greatest problem for the human race, to the solution of which Nature drives man, is the achievement of a universal civic society which administers law among men.

Again, the articulation of the telos, now expressed quite succinctly as "a universal civic society," is clear, but its achievement is set up as a problem. Indeed, the sixth thesis states: "This problem is the most difficult and the last to be solved by mankind."

It is presented as a "problem" because what moves us towards the goal is *conflict*, which Kant rearticulated as "unsocial sociability." Why does Kant say that this "problem" is "the last to be solved by mankind"? What does he mean by "the last" problem? The reason that the realization of the telos is the "last problem to be solved by mankind" is because, in a sense, the problem *is* mankind. When the problem of creating a "universal civic society" has been solved, we will have, in effect, transcended the condition of humanity itself. Why? Because, for Kant, what makes human beings the creatures that they are is that they are *willful*, that is, they are not directed to their ends by anything other than themselves—they must will themselves towards the ends that present themselves. What this means is that human beings always tend to be *self-interested*, directing themselves to those ends that they believe, for whatever reasons, best serve their own interests.

That in itself is not the principal problem, however. Kant speculated, as we have seen, that Nature "herself" had willed this in human beings because it is evident that the pursuit of self-interest has yielded a paradoxically productive context for developing human capacities. It is in my self-interest to work harder to achieve better results for myself, which at the same time, through that which is produced by the harder work, ameliorates conditions for others. Indeed, it can quite easily be seen that the creation and sustenance of a lawful social order can be in one's self-interest, even when that social order places limits on what one is allowed to willfully do. Paying taxes limits my disposable income, but my taxes pay for the police who protect me. The problem here is the dependence of "mankind" on willfulness itself. Because human beings are willfully directed towards their ends, they are just as likely to fail to appreciate what is truly in their (longer-term) self-interest, and to direct themselves to *particular* interests that merely satisfy passing whims and fancies or, worse, to submit that willfulness to the passions of the moment. Human beings are capable of rationality, although again this, for Kant, means understanding the lawfulness that governs the general processes of nature. However, this is a capacity that needs to be exercised, and human beings tend not to exercise it when other more forceful and/or enticing ends attract their attention. In other words, the willfulness of human beings, instead of being directed towards their own good as well as the good in general, often merely allows itself to be guided by inclination, by unreflective desire and attraction, or submits itself to its passions.

It is not my intention to get into Kant's general moral theory here. My concern is strictly with his speculative philosophy of history. Specifically, I am concerned with evaluating the way in which he links the telos he articulates so forcefully with the dynamics he develops much less seriously. In other words, while many still hold today to the telos that Kant articulated, namely, the constitution of a universal civic society, they have abandoned his attempt to connect it with the dynamics of social conflict generating the increased development of human capacities, and instead concentrate their energies on articulating as clearly as possible the normative framework that will help us deal with the world and the conflicts that flare up within it.

Like Kant, many believe that the articulation and implementation of such a framework will take time and effort on the part of individuals and nations across the globe. These efforts find expression in such instruments as the Universal Declaration of Human Rights, whose purpose is, as Axel Honneth says (in his paper "Is Universalism a Moral Trap?", p. 173), to place "the prohibitions and precepts codified in international law . . . above the basic rights codified in the individual nations," in an attempt to articulate the telos of a *universal* civic society. That such a universal civic society is still far from being realized in actuality is not something that deters those cosmopolitans who insist on the ideal. Without explicitly referring, as Kant does, to a secret plan of Nature that is moving us towards that ideal, they do claim that something like the Universal Declaration of Human Rights, as Honneth puts it (p. 170), "initiated an uninterrupted endeavour to make universal rights legal rights by creating internationally recognized instruments of complaint, control, and sanctions."

In terms of speculative philosophy of history, we might still ask how we are to understand the historical dynamics that are to draw us, albeit asymptotically, to the ideal. What do contemporary cosmopolitan idealists put in the place of Kant's "unsocial sociability"?

Different candidates might be considered, but a key feature in the developmental picture of contemporary cosmopolitanism—and here too they continue to follow Kant—is the emphasis on education. There is a conviction that the kinds of conflicts that tear the world apart, rather than those that foster further development, will be attenuated with the spread of education. We are not speaking here of an education into a particular doctrine or cultural point of view. Cosmopolitanism, because it seeks to grasp the world in its entirety from a universal point of view, needs a more abstract conception of education. It finds one in the idea of literacy, or education for literacy, or the elimination of illiteracy.

Emmanuel Todd, for example, has predicted in his *After the Empire* (p. 25) that the planet will achieve "universal literacy" by the year 2030. (*After the Empire* is an especially interesting work, given the objections raised to the way in which, in Todd's view, the United States, in its interventionist policies, is flaunting the cosmopolitan ideal. Todd argues that such "imperialist" ambitions, and indeed the notion that a single superpower can reign supreme, cannot be sustained.) For Todd the spread of literacy across the surface of the planet has had and will have important consequences. It even suggests to Todd a kind of "end of history" inasmuch as he predicts that global literacy will promote global stability through more balanced demographic development, evidenced in the spread of lower birth rates, which Todd claims will lead to an increased number of political regimes tending towards liberal democracy. His basic argument (pp. 45–46) runs as follows:

> Learning to read and write brings each person to a higher level of consciousness. The fall of birth rates is a prime system of these deep psychological changes. Thus, given the universal tendency toward complete literacy and demographic equilibrium, it is not illogical to witness a rapid proliferation of more democratic political regimes. One could advance the hypothesis that individuals who have been made conscious and free through literacy cannot be governed indefinitely in authoritarian ways; or, what amounts to the same thing, the practical costs of exerting authoritarian rule over a critically aware population render the society in which they live economically uncompetitive.

Todd thinks that both the increase in literacy and the spread of lower birth rates, largely as a function of increased literacy, will of themselves create a more stable world on the model of contemporary liberal democracies. The link between literacy and lower birth rates is explained quite simply (p. 27): "Once man, or more precisely women, know how to read and write, birth control can begin." Once birth rates are stabilized, then, in combination with literacy, human lives can move beyond the necessities of basic survival, and people can devote increased energies to different forms of spiritual and material development.

This should not be conceived as a smooth process. Literacy also can be seen at the heart of demographic displacements. As Todd observes (p. 27):

> We must keep in mind the importance of education when it comes to understanding the present wave of migration to Europe and the United States. Individuals who are rushing to get through the guarded gates of the richest countries are no doubt trying to escape from the material misery that still exists in the world's poorest countries. But their desire to flee this misery also reveals a higher level of sophistication in their aspirations that is the direct result of substantial increases in basic literacy attained in

their home countries. The consequences of education are innumerable. One of them is the psychological disorientation of populations.

Such "disorientation" itself can appear to be very disruptive of the otherwise "uninterrupted" progressive process of development that cosmopolitans point to and celebrate. As Todd acknowledges (p. 33):

> Progress is not, as Enlightenment thinkers may have believed, a pleasurable linear ascent on all fronts. Being uprooted from one's traditional life—from the well-trodden routines of illiteracy, pregnancy, poverty, sickness, and death—can at first produce as much suffering and disorientation as it does hope and opportunity. Very often, perhaps in a majority of cases, the transformation of cultural and personal horizons is experienced as social and individual crisis. Destabilized peoples behave violently both among themselves and toward others. The move into modernity is frequently accompanied by an explosion of ideological violence.

We may leave aside for the moment the unnecessarily uncharitable description of "traditional life" as well as the simplification of "Enlightenment thinkers." (We have seen that Kant, for one, could not be further from the view that progress should be understood as a "pleasurable ascent." On the contrary, the point of trying to think this notion of progress requires seeing the ascent *despite* the appearances that suggest otherwise, which is exactly what Todd is doing here.) Todd is pointing to an important feature of our societies that demonstrates the relevance of considering the wider framework of a developmental whole emphasized by speculative philosophy of history.

We have already discussed what Todd is here calling "the psychological disorientation of populations" when we mentioned the particular characteristic of a world that is "becoming increasingly multicultural" in terms of presenting both familiarities and "unfamiliar familiarities," that is, ways of living that might be strange or unfamiliar to me, but nevertheless share a social space that I remain committed to. (Remember the distinction between a "foreign" language spoken by someone who is considered a "foreigner" and the same language spoken by someone who is considered a fellow citizen.) The cosmopolitan idealist will insist that dealing with such "psychological disorientation" requires—you guessed it—more education.

That is fine and good, but considerations of education cannot forever stay at the abstract level of rates of literacy, the capacity to read and write. As Todd himself writes near the end of his book, the spread of literacy and the decline in birth rates, while they may point to the extension of democratic institutions and structures, do not produce an "education" that necessarily points to an increasing egalitarianism, or a greater recognition of the equal worth of all. Indeed, when Todd looks at industrialized and industrializing democracies alike, he concludes (p. 196) that they are being

> encroached on to varying degrees by a tendency towards oligarchy—a phenomenon that has emerged with the development of educational stratification that has divided societies into layers of "higher," "lower," and various kinds of "middle" classes.

Apparently unperturbed by this, Todd immediately goes on to say that:

> we must not exaggerate the anti-democratic effects of this inegalitarian educational stratification. Developed countries, even if they become more oligarchical, remain literate countries, and will have to deal with the contradictions and conflicts that could arise between a democratically leaning literate mass and university-driven stratification that favours oligarchical elites.

We have here an expression of the cosmopolitan's "faith." Both Parts Two and Three of this book will try to address a little more systematically the reasons for thinking through such "contradictions and conflicts," rather than merely affirming one's faith in the face of them. What we need to address is how the "disorientation" that is the result of the mixing and mingling of populations and provenances requires a "reorientation" that goes beyond, or deeper than, the promise of the "stability" of a liberalized world order.

To put it in the terms of speculative philosophy of history—and in terms of the question of where we are headed, given the increasingly multicultural character of the world—what we need to do is look more closely at the dynamics of the historical process, both in terms of the "disorientation" it provokes and the reorientation that those dynamics may be effecting in concrete terms, as these are illuminated by the explicit telos of a single shared world. In other words, cosmopolitans have successfully argued for the relevance of the telos of history, a universal civic society, but the account of the dynamics that animate the realization of the telos in concrete terms needs to be considered more carefully. Otherwise, we run the risk ultimately of banishing the telos from the real historical process, holding it up merely as an ideal to be either admired or reviled. To do so is a mistake, arising from having paid insufficient attention to the concrete dynamics of history, thus far identified as conflict and the attempt to resolve conflicts.

If the point of speculative philosophy of history is to make sense of the historical process, considered as a whole in terms of its telos *and* its dynamics, then we need to draw closer together the articulation of the telos and the understanding of the dynamics of history. Indeed, it can be argued that the telos needs to be seen as arising out of the dynamics of history, as opposed to being postulated as an asymptotic ideal meant to guide our understanding, or at least our appreciation, of those dynamics. This will be the essential move made by Hegel's speculative philosophy of history.

Before we turn to Hegel, we need to be clear about what has been achieved by considering Kant and the cosmopolitan point of view. Kant enables us to see the extent to which thinking about human development within the context of a "universal history," history considered as a whole, means thinking about human beings as essentially willful creatures, that is, as creatures who do not exist in the world as guided by instinct, but by their own appreciation and understanding of what the world is, given the way it presents itself to them. For Kant, that willfulness should be guided by a rationality capable of expressing the world in terms of *lawfulness*, both in nature and in the moral maxims that should govern one's conduct. Yet it must be remembered that even such rationality, or the exercise of such rationality, rests on our basic and essential willfulness as human beings. (Such willfulness is usually expressed by pointing to the freedom of human beings, their free will, but I shall reserve for the moment the use of the concept of freedom.) We may exercise that willfulness badly, allowing ourselves—our wills—to be pushed this way or that, with little resistance or thought on our part. It nevertheless remains the case that it is our wills— ourselves as wills, as willful—that are pushed and prodded in this way. It is this willfulness that is both the subject and object of history, considered as a whole. History is both that which our willfulness produces, these particular ways of life as opposed, and sometimes in opposition, to these other ways of life, *and* that which produces our willfulness. Each of us, as a natural being, is born into a cultural world and is either recognized and brought up into it, becoming a willful being and contributing in however small a way to the overall historical process, or left to die.

What Kant has also allowed us to see is that to truly understand this process of history understood as a whole we need to see it as governed by a telos, which he articulates in terms of our willfulness being guided by the regulative ideal of a "universal civic community," or, to cite his eighth thesis once again, "a perfectly constituted state as the only condition in which the capacities of mankind can be fully developed." Kant has made us focus on the *universality* of the historical process. However, that universality, articulated "from a cosmopolitan point of view," has been affirmed quite abstractly, especially as far as the dynamics of history are concerned. Whether it be a basic "unsocial sociability" or the spread of literacy, such conceptions do not give a firm enough grip on the dynamics of the historical process. No wonder, then, that it slips away from us, and all we are really left with is our faith in our guiding telos!

Fortunately, we do not have to leave things at that. We do not need to remain content with a merely abstract universality. What we need to recognize in dealing with cosmopolitan thinkers and speculative philosophers of history is that there is reason to think that we all belong to a single intelligible process that encompasses the whole of the world, and, that despite appearances, that process describes a progressive development. For those who still "instinctively" balk at such an idea, and in particular for those who think of the dismal history of violence, this development is not to be understood as a necessary one. Within the terms of the modal square (discussed in the Introduction to this book), we need to understand such progressive development as possibility inherent in the real as we encounter it.

However, as critics of cosmopolitan thinking point out, no one actually lives "in" the whole world. Human beings live lives in particular localities, even when they spread those lives out over different localities. Nevertheless, our contemporary cosmopolitan world does display increased mobility and much more flexible ties to particular localities. This increased mobility is relatively recent. Eric Hobsbawm expresses this quite well in his *The Age of Revolution: 1789–1848* when he writes (p. 25) that in 1789 the world was,

> for most of its inhabitants, incalculably vast. Most of them, unless snatched away by some awful hazard, such as military recruitment, lived and died in the county, and often in the parish, of their birth: as late as 1861 more than nine out of ten in seventy of the ninety French departments lived in the department of their birth. The rest of the globe was a matter of government agents and rumour.

The point is even more powerfully stated by Michel Serres in his *Hominescence*: that the cosmopolitanism evidenced by our mobility, and by the detachment from the localities of our births that characterizes the way we now inhabit the Earth, is manifest in what Serres calls the greatest and profoundest change in humanity since the Neolithic era, the biotechnological transformation of agriculture resulting in the evacuation of the "countryside." Because Serres is as much a poet as a philosopher, I shall cite him in his own words (p. 111, my translation):

> Here then is the greatest event of the twentieth century: the end of agriculture, inasmuch as it modelled conduct and cultures, the sciences, social life, bodies, and religions. No doubt farmers will continue to provide nourishment to their contemporaries; however, their gestures and their existence no longer steer humanity, no longer incite a humanism, no longer permit a framing of space and time. The West has just changed worlds. The Earth, understood as the planet photographed in its entirety by astronauts, takes the place of the earth, understood as this patch of

land laboured daily. This break separates the end of the last century from the whole of the past to Neolithic times; it has already transformed our relations to fauna, flora, the seasons, passing time, passing weather, bad weather, to the spaces we occupy, and to our habitat and displacements. It has changed our social ties: we no longer live together in the same way once we have effaced the nourishing ties linking the fields, resources, pastures and beasts, our occupation of a space, our defending it and going to war. We no longer even die in the same way, given that, preferring to burn them for lack of space in our cities, we no longer bury our dead in the soil mixed with the sweat of our labour.

We now live in cities and move between them, and it is within cities that one experiences in a very concrete way the basic idea of cosmopolitanism, that of all of us belonging to one world and of the world being one. Yet, at the same time, what this one world reveals to each of us, in a very concrete and immediate and quotidian way, are the differences that traverse the unity of the world.

In order to make sense of both the unity and the diversity of the world, we need to move beyond the affirmation of an abstract universality. If we are to speak of a "universal civic society," we need to ask what we mean by "universal." Étienne Balibar, in a paper entitled "Ambiguous Universality," addresses this question by distinguishing different modalities of the concept of universality. If we relate this to the observation that is at the heart of this book, namely that the world is "becoming increasingly multicultural," then Balibar enables us better to grasp concretely the paradox that an increasingly multicultural world exhibits itself increasingly as one world.

Balibar defines one kind of universality as real universality, or universality as reality—in my terms, universality as experienced in contact. Balibar says (p. 48) that this real universality manifests itself in the

> actual interdependency between the various "units" which together build what we call the World: institutions, groups, individuals, but also, more profoundly, the various processes which involve institutions, groups, and individuals: the circulation of products and persons, the political negotiations, the juridical contracts, the communication of news and cultural patterns, etc.

This interdependency needs to be understood both extensively, as applying, increasingly, across the globe, and intensively, as different parts of the world are increasingly dependent on the other parts. More important for our discussion here is that, for Balibar, this intensive aspect could be expressed by saying that interdependency is reaching the individual himself/herself in a direct manner, not only through the institutions or communities to whom he/she belongs.

What Balibar is saying is that it is increasingly the case that the interdependency of the world is being felt directly in the ways in which individuals actually experience their own lives. He uses as examples (p. 50):

when every individual's wage and skill become dependent on competitors anywhere on the world market, but also when educational curricula must include the learning of international languages, or sanitary regulations must control the individual's food and sexual habits because of the spread of world-epidemics (AIDS) . . .

What Balibar is pointing out, and it is a point I wish to emphasize, is that there is a concrete sense in which the telos of the cosmopolitan idealists, the realization of a "universal civic society," has already taken place. We already do live in a "universal civic society," in the sense that we all depend on one another in very real terms, as the arguments around the positive and negative impacts of "globalization" constantly remind us. To recognize this is to recognize the limitation of the cosmopolitan idealist point of view that postulated its telos asymptotically, as an end forever approached but never actually achieved. Of course, the cosmopolitan ideal of a universal civic society was meant as a moral ideal that would enable us to measure the real, and this required preserving the ideal from the real, which cosmopolitans understood as being in need of improvement. What they did not and, indeed, could not count on was that the real would catch up with the ideal, effectively creating a "universal civic society" in real, concrete terms. That is, as Balibar insists (p. 50) against what he considers to be the "utopian" thrust of the cosmopolitan ideal, we need to acknowledge

that real universality, or globalization, already achieves the goal which was conceived as "the unification of mankind," albeit certainly not implementing most of the moral (or "humanistic") values which utopias believed should be either a pre-condition or an immediate consequence of this unification.

This is to acknowledge that this real universality is not all that it has been cracked up to be. The world is far from realizing the conditions that would enable the full development of all human capacities, which, along with the realization of a universal civic society, also describes the telos of history as articulated "from a cosmopolitan point of view." In other words, the real has not completely swallowed up the ideal. There is still a need to distinguish a "real universality," which has in effect taken place, and in which the dynamics of history have caught up with its telos, from our remaining sense of a better world to come, which fuels a different sense of universality, called "ideal universality."

I fully recognize that many people actually give up at this point and give in to a sense of the "real" as exhausting any possibility of realizing ideals. They call themselves "realists" in order precisely to oppose "idealists." Clearly, I think that one should not succumb to such a temptation, otherwise I would not be writing this book. More importantly, I think that such a move towards a "realism" that opposes itself to an "idealism" is actually a mistake, both a logical and an existential mistake. It is a move that does not fully appreciate the modal square within which our lives unfold. In that sense, it is similar to the mistake of projecting the necessities of the past onto the future. There are no necessities in the future, since, by definition, the future is possibility because it is grounded in the contingency of our being faced with it. Remember, none of us had to exist, but we do, and in the particular ways that we do. We cannot change that which has contributed to those particular ways, because they are past. Those contributions are therefore necessary, but they remain grounded in the contingent fact of our continued existence in the present that faces the possibilities of the future. What "realists" are right to insist on is that those possibilities are structured in very real ways that cannot simply be wished away or ignored. Yet this is to say that possibilities are formed against the backdrop of impossibilities, themselves arising out of a structured past. If we are to think in terms of ideals and the realization of ideals, then we must take into consideration the impossibilities that the world presents to us, given the necessities of the past. That, however, is just another way of saying that only real possibilities realize themselves, which, of course, is redundant. Articulating the ideal should be understood as the attempt to make sense of these real possibilities of the world as it contingently exists for us.

We have reason, then, to maintain a distinction between the real and the ideal. However, we should not be too quick to relate real universality and ideal universality in a way that would merely repeat the cosmopolitan idealist view that the ideal should be preserved from the real in order to measure it. This would be to ignore the historical process, which has had real universality take over that ideal. This is Balibar's point: history shows that we now already do live in a "universal civic society." It is not the ideal society that we once upon a time wished for, but that is not surprising given that that ideal was set up as a (perpetual) wish, to inspire us. Now that that ideal has been overtaken by the real, what are we to do? That is the question that we need to address and that I have formulated in terms of responding to the question of where we are headed.

In order to address this question we need to be clear, or as clear as possible, about what is meant by the notion that "the real has overtaken the ideal." We have said, following Balibar, that the world manifests a real universality through both extensive and intensive interdependencies. The different parts of the world depend on each other for their development, *and* our own individual lives develop and unfold interdependently. What Balibar enables us to conceptualize is our sense that the world is "becoming increasingly multicultural" in a more systematic way.

To say that the world is becoming "increasingly" multicultural is another way of expressing the increasing *interdependence* of cultural realities. In order to get clear on what is meant by interdependence, we can again follow Balibar and contrast this notion of interdependence with that of a more familiar relationship of straight dependence between cultures, described in terms of majority and minority. It is probably easier to do this if one adopts the point of view of a minority culture. Anyone who has grown up in what is defined as a minority culture understands quite clearly the dependent relation that one's culture has with the self-defining majority culture. This relation of dependence is less evident for the majority culture, which, because it is self-defining, tends to view itself merely as a "culture," at least when things are running smoothly. Dependence is precisely what defines it as a minority.

If I take myself as an example, belonging to the French-speaking minority in the province of Manitoba was a consequence of being defined, and identifying myself, as depending on the surrounding majority English-speaking society for the continued conditions of my existence as a French-speaker. I was not a member of the French-speaking minority because there were relatively fewer French-speakers around me than English-speakers. In fact, on any given day, despite the fact that French-speakers formed only about six percent of the population of the province in which I lived, the great majority, not to say the totality, of the persons around me were French-speakers (for example, in school or in church). The fact that most of the people who surrounded me in most of my activities were nevertheless identified, and identified themselves, as a minority was a function of the way in which those activities were sustained both by and against the "majority." This is precisely what describes a relation of dependence. The dependence expressed itself in myriad institutional ways, but if we take the example of schooling, schools for French-speakers in the province existed only out of a sustained struggle to maintain the "minority rights" that were originally recognized in the Act of the Canadian Parliament establishing Manitoba as a province.

Another, more subtle, way in which this dependence was expressed was the fact that most of the French-speakers also learned to speak English at a fairly early age and in a way that rendered the speaking of it almost indistinguishable from the way the majority spoke it. This ability to switch from one language to another, which occurred either more or less unselfconsciously in the schoolyard, or illegitimately within the school, where official rules prohibited it, only accentuated the minority status and dependence of French-speakers on the unquestioned status of the English-speaking majority. Thus, there came into being the situation, a strange one on its face, of French-speakers who both were and were not English-speakers as well, where the ability to speak a particular language was not in itself sufficient or appropriate for one to consider oneself a speaker of that language.

It is this last point that is the most interesting for our discussion here. Of course, it was, and is, not uncommon for French-speakers-who-also-speak-English-but-are-not-English-speakers to gradually abandon the speaking of French in order to become English-speakers. In order to be recognized as an English-speaker one cannot also be a French-speaker (thus demonstrating the dependence of the minority of French-speakers on the English-speaking majority). While, from the perspective of French-speakers, those who abandon French-speaking in favour of exclusive English-speaking are deemed to be "assimilated," from the perspective of English-speakers such former French-speakers are recognized merely as members of the majority, with a particular ethnic history and background, but they are no longer recognized as a "minority" in any kind of substantial sense. From the perspective of the former French-speakers themselves, one sees oneself neither as a (former) member of a "minority" nor especially as a member of the "majority," one merely regards oneself as independent, something like a Member of Parliament who leaves his or her party without crossing over to another party. Of course, the children of former French-speakers, themselves having never spoken French, quite easily regard themselves, and continue to be regarded by others, as members of the majority.

I am, of course, describing a relation of cultural dependence that has defined (for a time) a particular context (the province of Manitoba within Canada). However, this context, like the rest of the world, is "increasingly becoming multicultural," which means that the relations of dependence established between minorities and majorities are being destabilized, not only through the multiplication of minorities, but also through the mixing of minorities that issues from the increased coexistence of minorities. That is, the increasing interdependence that characterizes the relations that constitute the world has as a consequence, to borrow Balibar's term, "blurred" the distinction between the majority and its minorities. This expresses itself in the fact that, as Balibar puts it (p. 53), "a growing number of individuals and groups are not easily inscribed in one single ethnic (or cultural, linguistic, even religious) identity." Indeed, as Balibar also points out, part of what it means to say that the world is "becoming increasingly multicultural" is to say that

> more individuals are not classifiable: marrying partners from different "cultures" and "races," living across the fictitious boundaries of communities, experiencing a divided or multiple "self," practicing different languages and memberships according to the private and public circumstances.

In such a context it is no longer clear what a "minority" is, given that there is no clear relation of dependence on a "majority."

Many people are prepared to celebrate this situation as a new dawn, heralding the day when the relations of dominance implied in the majority/minority distinction can finally be overcome. That would be premature. If increasingly multicultural relations do describe the "real universality" of the world, we should recall that it is far from ideal. As Balibar writes (p. 56):

> Real Universality is a stage in history where, for the first time, "Humankind" as a single web of interrelations is no longer an ideal or utopian notion but an actual condition for every individual; nevertheless, far from representing a situation of mutual recognition, it actually coincides with a generalized pattern of conflicts, hierarchies, and exclusions. It is not even a situation in which individuals virtually communicate with each other, but much more where global communication networks provide every individual with a distorted image or stereotype of all the others, either as "kin" or as "aliens," thus raising gigantic obstacles before any dialogue. "Identities" are less isolated and more incompatible, less univocal and more antagonistic.

Another way to describe the implications of the "Real Universality" of our contemporary world is to speak, as Alain Touraine does in his book *Can We Live Together?*, of a process of *demodernization*, which is engaged now that "modernism" through globalization has spread and covers the entire planet. The universality that globalization has achieved describes a reality that does not model itself on the gradual expansion of the smaller local societies in which we grow up and get to know the "world." On the contrary, according to Touraine (pp. 1–2), the universality established by globalization is one that detaches itself from the lived world of a particular social organization, such as the network of families, schools, and church that organized my French-Canadian upbringing not so very long ago, into a variety of "flows" or "networks" that spread across the planet:

Globalization means that technologies, instruments and messages are present everywhere, or, in other words, that they belong nowhere. They are not bound up with any one society or culture, as we can see from the ever-popular images that juxtapose petrol pumps and camels, Coca-Cola and villages in the Andes, jeans and royal palaces. The divorce between networks and collectivities, the indifference of the signs of modernity to the slow work of socialization that was once undertaken by families and schools—or in a word, the desocialization of mass culture—means that we live together only to the extent that we make the same gestures and use the same objects, but we cannot communicate with one another except by exchanging the signs of modernity. *Our culture is no longer in control of our social organization, and our social organization is no longer in control of technological and economic activity* [my emphasis]. Culture and the economy have become divorced from one another, as have the instrumental world and the symbolic world.

Touraine does not mean merely to note this "divorce" between culture and the economy, he aims to describe it in terms of its particular dynamics. It is the dynamics of an increasing separation between cultural self-understanding and economic activities that Touraine calls a process of *demodernization*. As we have seen, certain people are wont to declare "the end of history," in the sense that the world has become one world through a singular system of economic exchange whose workings promote increasingly democratic systems of government. We also saw that this one world is, for others, a world that will increasingly become one wracked by conflicts generated by the clash of cultural or "civilizational" differences. Touraine takes up these two competing views and summarizes them (p. 25) as follows:

On the one hand, a unified economy with a unitary institutional framework; on the other, the fragmentation of cultural identities. It is impossible to choose between these interpretations, not only because they both jump to conclusions, but mainly because they both fail to see what is really happening. Two worlds are being dissociated: the world of technologies and markets and the world of cultures, the world of instrumental reason and that of collective meaning, that of signs and that of meanings. What lies at the heart of our experience at the end of the century is the dissociation of the economy and cultures, of exchanges and identities.

The idea of understanding our contemporary world and its "Real Universality" in terms of such a process of "demodernization" neatly captures the claim I made earlier that what our contemporary world reveals, from the point of view of speculative philosophy of history, is that the dynamics of history have effectively taken over the telos. If, on Kant's view, the dynamics of history were to be understood as a kind of productive "unsocial sociability," and the telos of the process of history considered as a whole was to be understood as the progressively defined realization of a "universal civic society," then what the actual course of history has brought about is the universal extension of that productive unsocial sociability, thus creating an effectively universal society that, because it is driven by such *unsocial* sociability, can sustain a telos only by *preserving it from that universal society*. The ends to which we direct our lives are separated off from the economic activities that otherwise constitute our shared world.

Thus, one way to see the contemporary world is to see it as a worldwide sphere of economic activity, in which we all participate and compete, and from which we retreat in order to sustain frameworks of meaning and significance, more sociable networks structured around shared values, commitments, and mutual recognition. A consequence of this is that the world we live in, the world as we experience it, what is sometimes called the "lifeworld", according to Touraine (p. 41):

> no longer has any unity, not because contemporary society is too complex and is changing too fast, but because its members are affected by centrifugal forces which draw them, on the one hand, towards instrumental action and the attractive symbols of globalization and a modernity which is increasingly defined by desocialization and, on the other hand, towards an "archaic" membership of a community defined by the fusion of society, culture, and personality.

Thus we come back to Balibar's statement, quoted above, that within Real Universality "identities" are less isolated *and* more incompatible, less univocal *and* more antagonistic.

However, all of this is from the limited point of view of Real Universality. Of course, we cannot ignore this reality. It is what we live in contact. However, if we remind ourselves of the framework in which our lives unfold, that is, the past-present-future complex, then that contact with the reality of the present, defined here in terms of the Real Universality of the world, is structured by our knowledge of the past and the necessities it confronts us with—if we use Touraine's language, a process of demodernization that splits those lives into contributions to communicative and economic activities, and retreats into spheres of meaning and significance— as well as our future anticipations, understood as the possibilities that are filtered through existing impossibilities.

Our focus on our present world as Real University has been a focus on the present as structured by the past, in the attempt to give more substance to what it means to say that the world is "becoming increasingly multicultural," but we have not yet found a satisfactory answer to the question of where we are we headed. That is, given this increasingly multicultural world structured in terms of Real Universality, what are our expectations and anticipations of the future? What are they and how do we fold them back into our lives?

I said above that, if we stay within the parameters of Kant's speculative philosophy of history, then we can say that the dynamics of history have effectively taken over its telos by actually achieving a "universal society." This was never supposed to happen in Kant's account, because the whole point of articulating a telos was to provide an ideal, a standard with which to judge what we are trying to do in history and to enable us to evaluate our accomplishments as either successes or failures. This has led most thinkers to abandon Kant's speculative philosophy of history and to focus their attention on formulating normative frameworks with which to evaluate our varied attempts to live out our lives together.

However, in abandoning Kant's speculative philosophy of history, they have also abandoned his attempt to think the dynamics of history in terms of the telos by showing how they are linked. Given the Real Universality that characterizes our world, I think that this is a mistake. We are in great need of understanding how the dynamics of history are linked to the telos of history. Rather than completely abandon speculative philosophy of history, we should entertain the possibility that, having set it up in a very fruitful manner, Kant nevertheless got the relationship between the dynamics of history and its telos wrong. The particular way in which he got it wrong was to insist that the ideal as articulated in the telos serves only to guide and to judge what happens within the unfolding of the real, and is not itself a function of the real. What the actual unfolding of history has revealed to us, however, is that the real has overtaken the ideal, in that ideals themselves get folded back into our particular lives, while the universality they were meant to uphold actually belongs to the historical development of the world.

What we need now is not an abandonment of a mode of thought that attempts to think the relation between the dynamics of history and that which guides it, but a speculative philosophy of history that will enable us to make sense of the way in which that relation has developed, so that we can see the telos emerging from the dynamics themselves. This is the way in which we shall characterize Hegel's speculative philosophy of history, which actually owes a great deal to Kant.

PART II

The Dynamics of

Recognition

On Hospitality and the Presence of Others

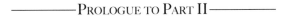

My mother once told me that her mother, out on the "homestead" in northern Saskatchewan, never refused a meal to a stranger showing up on the doorstep because that stranger might be Christ returned. I remember being surprised at the evangelical note struck by this story, which contrasted sharply with what I had experienced of my grandmother's otherwise quiet and ritualistic Catholic religiosity. Of course, the story also resonated because it confirmed a cliché about the Depression and the wandering souls, or "drifters," of the Prairies. However, I mention it here because this story has stuck with me as a kind of gauge of openness with regard to the presence of others.

I often ask myself, especially after I have refused yet again a request for a small donation from one of the sometimes cheerful, sometimes strangely morose canvassers at my doorstep, perhaps because they usually appear at suppertime, what I would do if the stranger at my door asked for food and shelter. Unlike my grandmother, I know I would find some way to refuse to honour the request directly, although, depending on the circumstances, I would perhaps provide some kind of assistance, such as use of the phone, directions to other, more official channels, perhaps a few dollars. Or perhaps not. Perhaps I would merely close the door with a nod and a smile, as I have so often before. It is difficult to know what I would do, of course, because of the unlikeliness of the particular request, especially considering that the question I ask myself is fed by particular images of the destitute lodged in my imagination. Even now the image that immediately comes to mind is that of a "drifter" at my doorstep, dusty and ragged clothes and all. That, of course, is the point. While my grandmother's preparedness to feed whatever stranger asked to be fed was certainly buttressed by the fact that she regularly fed any number of strange men who periodically appeared to help on the farm, and then disappeared, I have no reason to doubt that she would indeed have been open and committed to feeding that "complete stranger."

I have also often thought of that basic and fundamental openness and commitment when, driving as I do every week along some pretty deserted stretches of highway between Sudbury and Ottawa, I consider how I might be received if I trundled up the long, lonely lanes of the few houses I notice from the road to ask for assistance if and when my car broke down. I do have a cell phone, but coverage on some stretches of the highway is spotty at best, although, interestingly, it has improved in the past few years, confirming yet again the globalizing reach of our world. Especially in the dead of winter, on one of the dark, cold, sometimes late evenings that sometimes catch me on the road, I would like to think that the circumstances and relative isolation by themselves would create a situation that would make my appearance less easy to dismiss than that essentially similar appearance on my own front door in the suburbs. I am not sure, however, and I am somewhat disturbed by that uncertainty. That again is the point. What sense can we make of those situations that we find disturbing, for which no ready answer makes itself available? What happens when we focus on them? What do they reveal about the way our commitments and expectations operate in our thinking?

If I return to my example, is there any reason that I should expect to be received and helped with less hesitation by a person inhabiting an isolated house in a remote part of the country than I expect of myself when I contemplate someone on my doorstep in the suburbs? Aside from what this might say about me personally—which, I must admit, does not speak well for my altruistic inclinations when put on paper, though I am only trying to be honest—might there not be certain expectations built into these two situations that might say something about how expectations get folded into the very structuring of the way we work out our relations to others, especially when those others are strangers to us?

Apparently there are no statutes, at least in the common-law provinces of Canada, that impose a legal obligation to provide assistance to others. I cannot, therefore, have a legal expectation that I would be helped by anyone in one of the few houses I can see from the highway. Yet I retain a certain expectation that I would be helped, an expectation that, again, I do not extend to the suburban setting. Why? As I mentioned above, I drive down this stretch of highway every week and the isolated houses have become somewhat familiar to me over the years. I am also invariably surprised when I notice dwellings that I have not noticed before, usually in the winter when the canopy of leaves is not there to conceal them—dwellings further back from the road, or tucked away behind

MULTICULTURAL DYNAMICS AND THE ENDS OF HISTORY

rocks or copses. These unnoticed dwellings contrast quite sharply with those other dwellings that manifest themselves openly to the highway with its passing traffic, some of them delightfully strewn with coloured lights around Christmas. The driveways of the latter open invitingly out onto the highway and no doubt I would choose, if choice there was, one of those snow-blown driveways and brightly lit houses as a target for my solicitation if and when I needed help. Indeed, one might say that those particular houses, set close to the highway and in plain view, contribute to my expectation, because they are in fact *inviting* in their disposition. Some of them are even quite showy, and I have no doubt that my sudden appearance on the doorstep of one of them would be no cause for alarm. Especially after nightfall, the lights that shine from these houses appear as beacons of humanity in the surrounding wilderness. More than that: if these dwellings have been built so close to the highway and with such an evident opening out onto the highway, it is, no doubt, partly because they are affirming a link and connection to the flow of that highway. The driveway flows out onto the highway as much as the highway flows into these driveways, as tributaries flow from the main stream. If I am drawn to these particular dwellings, it is because they have disposed themselves as open to me.

Now, contrast this with a typical suburban streetscape, with its rows and bays and crescents of very similarly constructed houses bunched together on narrow lots. Although they can similarly be decked out at Christmas time and the snow is meticulously blown or shovelled off their driveways, their openness onto their streets is nowhere as *inviting* as those highway homes described above. Indeed, the very conception of twisting and turning the streets into crescents and bays is meant to discourage through traffic and the passing by of strangers, while the highway, of course—in my example, the *Trans*-Canada Highway—is meant to provide a route for those passing through. Consequently, the expectation that I might have of doors opening more than a crack or a head-width as my request for help is evaluated is quite different. Again, what I am pointing out here is not intended as a comment on the individuals who occupy any of these homes. Any given person might open their door wide and be extremely helpful in all kinds of ways. I am talking about the physical disposition of the homes themselves and what they can be said to manifest. Crowded together in the suburbs, these dwellings nevertheless affirm their privacy and independence. Indeed, though they may be built a mere body length apart from each other, they are advertised as "single" and "detached," and priced accordingly, each being meant to be the proverbial "castle" for its owner. This independence and the presupposition of privacy that such homes are meant to display are perhaps most succinctly expressed by the discreet manner in which a few of them display their willingness to be open to others by placing "Neighbourhood Watch" posters in their front windows.

I have devoted this much space to describing these two different types of dwelling in order to suggest that our expectations can be embodied in various ways and, in fact, can be very diffuse for the most part, only congealing, as it were, in particular contexts, such as would arise if and when my car broke down at night. If I can expect help from the isolated dwelling on the highway, it is because the very inhabitation in such a remote spot, but one nevertheless within sight of the main thoroughfare, itself signals a preparedness to receive such visitations. Again, a particular individual may refuse to recognize such an expectation on the part of the visitor, and I am not claiming that there is any kind of binding obligation upon them, only trying to point out that that individual would be mistaken to be *surprised* by such an expectation. In contrast, the suburban dwellings, in their somewhat forced "single" and "detached" independence, are constructed in such a way as to discourage such expectations, so that if perchance my car broke down on one of these crescents late in the evening, *I* should not be surprised if my solicitation was greeted with considerable suspicion, if not outright hostility. That is not to condone such hostility: I am merely concerned with the logic of expectation.

This discussion of the ways in which some of our expectations of helpfulness from others, or the lack of it, can be translated in terms of social space can be framed within a more general consideration of *hospitality*. Here we turn to another essay by Kant, "Perpetual Peace" (1795), in which he attempts to articulate and set out in a series of articles the basic rational tenets that would need to be understood and respected if peace among human beings is to be envisaged in any lasting sense. This piece is in many ways a continuation of the speculative effort in his "Idea of a Universal History from a Cosmopolitan Point of View." There, as we have seen, Kant argued for the telos of a "universal civic community," which, as he recognized in the seventh thesis of that essay, is "dependent upon the problem of a lawful external relation among states." "Perpetual Peace" can and should be read as contributing to the attempt to solve that problem.

The third of the "definitive articles for a perpetual peace" that Kant proposes in this essay states that: "The Law of World Citizenship Shall Be Limited to Conditions of Universal Hospitality." Kant means to move the question of hospitality away from mere sensibility, or an arbitrary dependence on particular dispositions, into the realm of legal recognition. He goes on to explain what he means by hospitality:

> Hospitality means the right of a stranger not to be treated as an enemy when he arrives in the land of another. One may refuse to receive him when this can be done without causing his destruction; but, so long as he peacefully occupies his place, one may not treat him with hostility. It is not the right to be a permanent visitor

MULTICULTURAL DYNAMICS AND THE ENDS OF HISTORY

that one may demand. A special beneficent agreement would be needed in order to give an outsider a right to become a fellow inhabitant for a certain length of time. It is only a right of temporary sojourn, a right to associate, which all men have. *They have it by virtue of their common possession of the surface of the Earth, where, as a globe, they cannot infinitely disperse and hence must finally tolerate the presence of each other. Originally, no one had more right than another to a particular part of the Earth* [my emphasis].

Kant's understanding of hospitality raises a number of interesting questions. Although it is clear that his own definition considers the hospitality that we owe others to be conditional, and that he would like to see the conditions for hospitality lawfully and rationally codified, his justification for considering hospitality at all can lend itself to an unconditional interpretation. That is, if it is the case that, "Originally, no one had more right than another to a particular part of the Earth," then one might say that the "original" condition of our relations to one another is an open one, in which no one has a particular claim against another for occupying exclusively a particular piece of the Earth's surface.

Of course, this "original" condition is not our actual one. Our actual condition is one that is structured in very specific ways, indeed in very specific legal ways. Yet the very specificity of these legal structures leads one to question their claim to be universal, applying to everyone equally. Laws are, after all, formulated by lawmakers in response to particular contingent circumstances and they are bound to reflect those circumstances. This is why we appeal to lawyers when we are faced with legal matters. We need them to help us interpret what the law is actually saying in its own peculiar language about our always particular situations.

Buying a house, for example—that is, in Kantian terms, making a claim to a particular piece of the surface of the Earth as constituting our home—is an elaborate, even arcane, process, the details of which many homeowners do not bother to master as long as they are suitably convinced that they are the legal "owners" of their home. What does it mean to be the "owner" of one's home? In the context of the foregoing discussion, it means that I am the one who decides who is allowed to enter it, to cross its threshold, as I open the door first a crack, then the width of a human face, then the width of human shoulders, and finally sufficiently wide to let a body pass through. Ownership, then, sets up the conditions of hospitality, or at least of *conditional* hospitality. As Meyda Yegenoglu argues (in her "Liberal Multiculturalism and the Ethics of Hospitality in the Age of Globalization") conditional hospitality is offered at the owner's place, home, nation, state, or city—that is, at a place where he is defined as the master and where unconditional hospitality or unconditional trespassing of the door is not possible. The host, the non-guest, the one who accepts, the one who offers hospitality, the one who welcomes, is the owner of a home and therefore is the master of the home.

At least, this is how things look when one attempts to codify both hospitality and ownership. However, one need not own a home in order to have one. If it is true that hospitality presupposes hosts in their home, absent explicit codification, their home might merely be demarcated by the space they occupy, a space that remains their space in the sense that they can expect to return to it after they have left it. Home is here understood as a "private" space where one finds shelter from the exigencies of a wider world, that space that Georges Duby describes, in *A History of Private Life* (Volume I, p. viii), as:

> a zone of immunity to which we may fall back and retreat, a place where we may set aside arms and armour needed in the public place, relax, take our ease, and lie about unshielded by the ostentatious carapace worn for protection in the outside world.

Such private spaces are constructed or, perhaps better stated, carved out of the world, sometimes with considerable difficulty and only relative success, at any stage of one's life.

Take, for example, a situation masterfully described by Anita Brookner in her most recent novel, *Leaving Home*. The passage in question describes an occasion when the protagonist, a young woman in her twenties, having met an older, recently divorced man at a party (the party having been arranged in part for precisely this purpose), is invited after dinner in a restaurant to have coffee in the man's home. The host leaves the room and the guest observes (p. 87):

> I took the opportunity of his absence in the kitchen to look round the room from which he was anxious to escape. I understood his reluctance to spend a Sunday afternoon here. It appeared to be half-furnished: perhaps his wife had carried off the more attractive pieces. The house was handsome enough in its flat-fronted way from the outside, but gloomy within. Dark stairs led up to this first-floor drawing-room, which seemed redolent of absence. Three widely spaced armchairs and a small round table were marooned on a hardwood floor, throwing into stark relief a set of unembellished shelves. Dull striped curtains, of an obviously expensive material, obscured much of the light, although the day had been sunny. Now I was aware of a chill which seemed not so much physical as emotional. Yet he was not obviously deprived; his conversation had if anything been bracing. I thought that he had made a respectable job of his semi-widowed state, and gave no sign of torment, though

that might have existed. It was not a room in which one was tempted to move about. Once assigned to a chair one would be inclined to wait there for further orders, as I did now.

Indeed, she takes her leave very soon after having her coffee, neither of them being ready to pursue their budding acquaintance within the context of a home that the legal owner is still in the process of "mastering." What I think this passage can be said to reveal is that, within any context of conditional hospitality that structures our interactions with others, there is also a sense of the basic openness and vulnerability to others that describes an unconditional hospitality or human openness to other humans based, in Kant's words, on our "common possession of the surface of the Earth," the surface upon which we are called to interact merely by the fact that we find ourselves here, at any particular time, and in the particular space we find ourselves occupying. In other words, an unconditional hospitality is one that acknowledges the basic vulnerability at the heart of our attempts to live out our own lives among others. That acknowledgement, perhaps epitomized in the taking into one's home of a newborn life, quickly becomes a structured set of particular norms and rules and ways that, ideally, are meant to shore up this essential vulnerability, but can never replace it.

My grandmother gave birth to ten children. I can hardly imagine what that means, although, of course, at the very least it meant feeding many mouths. Much of her life was given over to the feeding of those hungry mouths. The home she maintained and the time she lived in were built on an understanding of the importance of hospitality, but her particular openness to any stranger shows that she understood how the notion of hospitality in itself, as Jacques Derrida argued in his essay "Hospitality," is one that cannot sustain itself. It "implodes" by insisting on a conditionality that undermines it. Derrida writes (pp. 4–5):

> This is the principle, one could say the aporia, of both the constitution and the implosion of the concept of hospitality . . . Hospitality is a self-contradictory concept and experience which can only self-destruct <put otherwise, produce itself as impossible, only be possible on the condition of its impossibility> or protect itself from itself, auto-immunize itself in some way, which is to say, deconstruct itself—precisely—in being put into practice.

That is, by unconditionally opening her home to the "complete stranger," my grandmother was in effect not treating her home as a home, as a private space of immunity and self-preservation. If the door is always open, then there is no door and, if there is no door, than there is no hospitality. Or rather, as Derrida writes (p. 14):

> To take up the figure of the door, for there to be hospitality, there must be a door. But if there is a door, there is no longer hospitality. There is no hospitable house. There is no house without doors and windows. But as soon as there are doors and windows, it means that someone has the keys to them and consequently controls the conditions of hospitality. There must be a threshold. But if there is a threshold, there is no longer hospitality. This is the difference, the gap, between the hospitality of invitation and the hospitality of visitation. In visitation there is no door. Anyone can come at any time and can come in without needing a key for the door. There are no customs checks with a visitation. But there are customs and police checks with an invitation. Hospitality thus becomes the threshold or the door.

If I think again of my grandmother, she was quite literally leaving the door open for a "visitation," in her terms an otherworldly one, in my terms here one of basic and fundamental worldliness, of the basic fact of worldliness, that we all are born into a world that only then, if it accepts us, begins to shape us and that we attempt to shape. Whatever those shapes turn out to be—good, bad, powerful, lost, bored, troubled, troubling, erratic, inspiring, consistent, puzzling, ordinary, extraordinary—they presuppose and embody a basic openness to others. As Kant says, "Originally, no one had more right than another to a particular part of the Earth."

I have used these pages to discuss Kant, Derrida and my grandmother because they show, through their understanding of the notion of hospitality and its inherent limits, what lies at the heart of, and at the same time delimits, the notions of "culture" and "society" as these continue to be challenged by a world that is becoming increasingly multicultural. Such a world, a world of increasing migration and resettlement, challenges us to think anew what it means to claim to be "at home." Is it to defend a threshold? Or does it mean that we should be more willing to open our doors to those who find themselves outside? Or perhaps we are called upon to question and think anew the very notions of a "threshold" and of an "outside." As Kant says, the very fact that we inhabit a globe implies that we "cannot infinitely disperse and hence must finally tolerate the presence of each other." Is such tolerance the basic expectation that our increasingly multicultural world demands? Or might we not expect something more from recognizing the presence of each other?

3

Mutual Recognition and the Challenge of Unfamiliar Familiarities

The last two chapters focused on the question of where we are headed. This chapter and the following one will focus on the claim that the world is becoming increasingly multicultural. What I would like to do is describe what might be called the *dynamics* of multiculturalism. That is, I would like to argue that, if we want to try to understand our world as "multicultural," we must think through and with the coexistence of many different independent cultures sharing a common space or territory. While it is true that the world has always contained many different cultures, what our "multicultural" world points to is the close proximity, indeed, the quotidian coexistence of different cultures.

Having said that, we must admit that the concept of culture generated by the picture of "multicultural coexistence" is itself too abstract, too neat, or, put another way, too artificial. The relation that each of us maintains with "culture" is actually quite nebulous and diffuse, and our relation to a "multicultural" world is even more so. We need to recognize that the "multi-" in multicultural reality expresses the intermingling and quotidian interaction of different groups of people, and not the confrontation, peaceful or otherwise, of clearly demarcated cultural units. This is worth insisting on because it poses a challenge to our conventional ways of thinking about how the world divides itself. For example, Will Kymlicka implicitly recognizes this when, in his paper "Multicultural States and Intercultural Citizens," and elsewhere, he switches from using the "multi-" prefix in order to speak of *inter*cultural citizenship, dialogue, and communication, because he wishes to preserve the self-identity of the interacting cultural groupings. Yet a large part of the challenge of an increasingly multicultural world resides in the fact that the demarcations between cultural groupings are increasingly less well-defined.

Someone might want to point out here that I have said that we are talking about the intermingling and quotidian interaction of different *groups* of people. What demarcates and identifies these different groups, both as groups and as different, are cultural factors, are they not? Why not speak clearly and call these different groups "cultures," so that we can move on to the harder and more pressing work of determining how to ensure their peaceful and prosperous coexistence?

Such an approach is much too hasty and begs too many questions. More importantly, it fails to capture the dynamics of cultural identification, or cultural appropriation. The focus should not be on the different *groups* of people, understood as separate collectives, but on the intermingling and quotidian interaction that are manifested and result in more or less clearly demarcated *groupings* of people. It is through our quotidian interaction with each other that such groupings are formed and maintained. To put it in other terms, groupings are constituted by the repeated forms of *gathering together* that human beings engage in as they interact with one another.

What do we see when we focus on the dynamics of these interactions, and how are we to interpret what we see? I want to suggest that a fruitful approach would be to track, among these dynamics, the particular dynamic of what might be called *the familiar and the unfamiliar*. There are many ways of doing this. If one thinks of the various groupings that form and are manifested through our daily interactions with each other, when viewed from the inside as it were, the glue and attraction are the patterns of familiarity they exhibit. Of course, such patterns of familiarity are set against what is unfamiliar, hence the attraction.

One need only think of those professional gatherings called "meetings" or "conferences." One enters, scans the room for familiar faces, responds accordingly, and the response, varying from a slight nod to starting or joining a conversation, depends on, or is directly related to, the otherwise surrounding unfamiliarity. Or think about sitting in a restaurant in a country where you do not understand the language and then overhearing your own language being spoken at the next table. You immediately find yourself, not at home, but at least in less unfamiliar circumstances.

Thus, groupings manifest and constitute themselves through the recognition of familiarities. Now, if we focus our attention on our interaction with one another within a *multicultural* context, something interesting and, perhaps, novel, as far as the dynamics of human gathering are concerned, is revealed. A multicultural public space has the following distinctive feature: people are gathered in groups that are constituted, on the one hand, around the recognition of familiarities and, on the other hand, within a space that itself strives to recognize the coexistence of other groups constituting themselves around the recognition of *other* familiarities. That is, we might say that there are two dynamics of recognition at work within this multicultural space. Because it is a cultural space, one can see quite obviously that recognition of familiarities that is distinctive to particular cultures. However, because it is also a *multi*cultural space, there is the recognition from any given set of cultural familiarities of other, differing sets of cultural familiarities, which are then, by definition, unfamiliar. It is this second mode of recognition that is the distinctive feature of the multicultural space. It is one that fosters, to put it somewhat paradoxically, the recognition of *unfamiliar familiarities*. I say "unfamiliar familiarities" because what is being recognized is another distinct grouping constituted around a set of familiarities that one *also recognizes* as unfamiliar from the perspective of one's own set of familiarities.

What I am pointing to, then, is a distinct form of recognition. I use the seemingly contradictory expression "unfamiliar familiarity" because what is being recognized is neither that which is familiar nor that which is unfamiliar, but both at once. Or rather, and this is captured by the expression as well, we are indeed talking about a particular kind of familiarity, born of the particular kind of proximity afforded by our multicultural space of interaction, and characterized by the daily encounter with unfamiliar ways of rendering the world familiar.

Recall the everyday experience of riding the bus home from work or school seated next to a group of people, who are, perhaps, familiar from the workplace or from the campus, now speaking a language that one does not understand. Within a multicultural space such an experience does not typically carry with it the negative feelings of exclusion or fear—what are they saying? are they talking about me?—that often accompany experiences of unfamiliarity.

This goes against Will Kymlicka's generally negative reading of what he calls intercultural relations, which stand in need of *local* intercultural education, as opposed to the overprivileged preoccupation with what he calls *global* interculturalism. I think that Kymlicka's discussion here is seriously hampered by his switch to the "inter" prefix, which presupposes too neat a distinction and demarcation between cultures. His model remains one that privileges relations between what he calls "societal cultures," rather than the efforts of those committed to various groupings to live together within multiple cultures. My suggestion is that such negative feelings are absent because the unfamiliarity here is at the same time familiar. It is an unfamiliar familiarity.

This mode of recognition bears a family resemblance to the notion of "tolerance," in the sense that it accepts that public interaction needs to be respectful of basic differences between people. However, I would argue that, *as a form of recognition*, tolerance is deficient because it leaves the kinds of negative feelings that can accompany such encounters with the unfamiliar intact and, more importantly, as we shall see, it does not engage the unfamiliarity itself.

It is here that we will be able to address Kymlicka's desire to downplay the need for what he calls "deep mutual understanding," which he deems "utopian". In the paper I mentioned above Kymlicka writes (p. 165):

> the aim of intercultural education should not primarily be deep mutual
> understanding, but rather acknowledgement of the (partial) opaqueness of cultural
> differences, and hence the necessity for groups to speak for and govern themselves,
> and the necessity of finding ways of coexisting that can be accepted by all. This, I
> would suggest, is a more realistic goal, which lies in between the tokenist teaching
> of superficial cultural differences, and the utopian quest to understand deep cultural
> differences. Here again, the quest for a particular form of (deep) intercultural
> knowledge, rooted in a model of the ideal intercultural citizen, may go beyond,
> and perhaps even conflict with, the sort of intercultural relations required by a just
> multicultural state.

Kymlicka shows here that his primary theoretical concern is with the stability of the state form as a guarantor of just relations. My concern, however, is not with the state form itself but with understanding the multicultural dynamics that increasingly challenge it.

I would like to insist that unfamiliar familiarity is a distinct feature of multicultural societies as opposed to monocultural or traditional societies, that is, those societies whose extended social relations reflect or mirror familial relationships (a point made by John Russon in his book *Human Experience*, to which we shall return in a moment). Daily interactions in multicultural societies are structured around and include the encounter of both the familiar and the unfamiliar. In other words, there is in multicultural societies an implicit and irreducible recognition of the coexistence of different ways of rendering the world familiar. Of course, monocultural or traditional societies can also recognize that there are other ways of rendering the world out there familiar, but these different ways do not coexist.

This is how I think we should conceptualize what is often called "pluralism" in the context of contemporary societies, the idea that there are irreducibly different ways of living "good" lives. It is at the level of *the everyday* that this needs to be understood. We should not underestimate the importance of the everyday in understanding the dynamics of history and the multicultural dimension of history. The "multicultural" in history requires that we understand a particular social dynamic, one with its own characteristics, and to understand a social dynamic is to understand the structures of "everydayness" and the realities that such "everydayness" must confront.

Will Kymlicka doubts that we can achieve what he calls "full mutual understanding" and argues that, on the contrary, we should recognize an ineliminable "opaqueness" to the differences we encounter in others. That such opaqueness exists is no doubt true, but it should not be treated as a conclusion about the extent to which we can understand others around us. It should rather be treated as a premise, leading us to question not only the differences displayed by others, but also our own self-understanding as we encounter those others. This is because the opaqueness in the differences displayed by others is actually a kind of challenge posed to our own unreflective and familiar self-understanding, as this manifests itself in the structures of our everyday life. Indeed, this might be a good way to define what is meant by "everydayness." It describes the world as we habitually and unreflectively encounter it in our day-to-day activities, which is itself, in a certain way, *opaque even to ourselves.*

In this regard John Russon, following Heidegger, insists on the unreflective dimension of our being-in-the-world. In his paper "Hegel, Heidegger, and Ethnicity" he writes (p. 516):

> Becoming a member of society requires becoming habituated to a series of practices which *do* structure a dynamic of recognition along intelligible lines, but which *do not* appear as such to the practitioner; in other words, becoming a member of society—becoming self-conscious—really requires *not* knowing who one is, not knowing what it means to be a member of society, not being explicitly self-conscious in one's social identity.

The world, then, on this view, is opaque because it is the familiar world that we have literally grown up to recognize as our world, the world as it has accepted us and formed us, and given us our bearings and the sense of significance that carries us forward. It has the opaqueness of family life.

This is why it is important, when trying to understand the dynamics of social life, not to start either from the perspective of distinct individuals or from that of the social whole itself. Rather, we must look to the formation of selves within the context of familiar/unfamiliar others. In *Human Experience* (p. 65) Russon gives the following excellent account of the beginnings of such a formation of oneself:

> One's natural body is not an unbiased, universally uniform, fully transparent, or fully comprehensive accessing of reality, but is a perspectival, particular, opaque, and determinate hold on, posture in, and taste of being. We do not begin, as it were,

fully connected to reality, but have a particular opening, a particular clearing within which we can develop and expand, and the form in which we develop—the forms in which we transcend the limitations that initially define ourselves—are always shaped and figured by this original determinacy. The same is true of our initial participation in the reality of intersubjective life. We do not begin as full participants in a fully formed "we," but have, rather, a particular and determinate contact with others that is the arena within which we can establish routes for grasping, posturing ourselves in, and tasting human reality as such. We enter intersubjectivity through becoming familiar with particular others, and these familiars are our originary vision of intersubjectivity, of "who we are." It is our family—our group of familiars—that first defines for us where we fit into intersubjective relations and, consequently, what will count as the values by which "we" must approach the world, by which we must contact reality. Our family defines for us our proper place, and, indeed, the place of propriety—of value—itself.

However, even though the family provides the original context, our introduction to the world, by familiarizing us to an everydayness that can structure livable lives, the familiar world that it sustains does not exhaust our humanity, nor does it completely describe our contact with reality, which (as discussed in earlier chapters) is the way we experience the "present" within the past-present-future complex. In fact, our familiar world is in many ways a world that defines itself against this "contact" with a reality that surpasses it. However, this contact includes contact not only with what our familiarities do not comprehend, but, precisely, contact with "unfamiliar others." As Russon says (p. 67):

> Even as, for each of us, our family defines itself as the definitive sphere of human relations, it also has the function of opening us out onto other human situations. As much, then, as our identities are constitutively defined by a relation with familiar/familial others, our identities are constituted by an opening out onto non-familiar others. Emerging as a human subject is, thus, to be initiated into a world defined by a double openness of relations to familiars and relations to strangers.

This is especially true in an increasingly multicultural world. If families initiate us into the world, both by providing it with significance and by giving each of us a sense of what we are capable of within it—and, of course, different families do this differently and with different degrees of success—families also *contrast* with a wider, beckoning world, to be explored and discovered. We grow up within our families, but we also break away from them, even if only to eventually reconstitute ourselves within other families that maintain close relations with members of our original family, those who contributed to our original sense of the significance of the world and of our own significance within it—or not. This contrast Russon articulates as the contrast between family life and "transfamilial" *social* life, which displays a larger sense of the diversity of humanity, in the sense that what one encounters in this wider transfamilial social life is a wider diversity of ways of making sense of the world, of seeing its significance and the significance that one has within it.

Of course, this encounter with a wider diversity, especially in an increasingly multicultural world, is not abrupt or unexpected. After all, the adults in any particular family participate both in family life, with its developmental concerns, and already in a wider social world, which contains purposes and expectations not necessarily directed to the developmental concerns of family life (although of course, such purposes and expectations cannot be entirely alien to those concerns, insofar as social life is constituted around the activities of adults themselves generated by, and, for the most part, responsible for, particular families). In fact, as Russon argues, the contrast between family life and social life is a *dynamic* one that impacts on both the ways in which families are formed and the way in which the social world is organized, which in turn impacts on how one understands *oneself* as a developmental being attempting to live out one's life. Born within a family, one makes one's life in a social world. Russon writes (p. 71):

> It is as a social member that one is someone—that one can be *recognized* by one's others, and thereby recognize oneself, as someone—and the very capacity that one has to pose the issues of identity and so on is itself a product of participation in that society and its ritual structures of education into human identity. The difference between the phenomenon of the family and the phenomenon of the society is that within the family the familiar narrative into which one is born is automatically decisive, whereas in the society the ruling narrative can override familial narratives and, indeed, has as its particular function the *integrating of a multiplicity of families*. One's identity in the family is simply one's role as a member—son, mother, and so on—and as a representative agent of the family narrative. *One's identity in the society is as a single, equal adult, and as a representative of the transfamilial narrative* [my emphasis]. To become a member of a larger society, then, requires that one adopt a stance of *challenge* to the legitimacy of the family narrative.

Thus, on Russon's account, to "become a member of a larger society" essentially means to become an adult who, along with all other equal adults, is called upon to "represent" what he calls the "transfamilial narrative" that organizes and structures social life. What is required of adults is the ability to affect a "self-transcending critique" in their encounters with other adults, in such a way to promote forms of *mutual recognition*, which for Russon can also be understood as forms of what he calls (p. 60) "mutual education."

It is important to understand that what is meant by "self-transcendence" is the openness at the core of experience, that is, experience—or, better put, experiencing—is precisely this opening out onto and into a world. Now, to grasp why experience, understood developmentally, is self-transcending *critique*, we need to remember that experience is structured by that which is familiar *and* by that which is unfamiliar. Russon captures this dynamic between the familiar and the unfamiliar when he writes about the "figured contact" that describes the structure of experience. Interaction within the world is premised on a familiarity that, in effect, figures or configures our access to a sensible world. Yet that interaction is always also a *contact* with a *reality* that tests that familiarity. The unfamiliar is that which tests the familiar, that which demands of the familiar that it account for itself. Critique is precisely this accounting, the justification that familiarity gives of itself in view of its contact with the unfamiliar that describes social (and political) life, as opposed to family life, whose purpose is to provide a context for habituation and confirmation of one's ultimate significance and importance.

What I find particularly valuable in Russon's approach is the way in which it allows us to see how critique fails precisely when it fails to be "self-transcending," that is, when it fails to be open to the unfamiliarity that challenges its own familiarities, which remain necessary because they provide critique with its sense and direction. In other words, Russon allows us to see how critique must be both open and grounded—open to the unfamiliar, but grounded in the familiar. On the one hand, a critique that fails to be open to the unfamiliar is merely a turning away from "contact" with reality, a retreat into one's habitual world, with all the dysfunctions that such habituality can imply. On the other hand, a critique that fails to ground itself in its own familiarities is merely abstracting from reality, and constructing ideal and ideological worlds.

This can be illustrated with the recent—indeed, ongoing—question of the recognition of same-sex marriages. There are a considerable number of homosexual couples, and people who support them, who insist on having their unions recognized as marriages in the same way that many heterosexual couples have their unions so recognized. From within the groupings of those who are in favour of such a view, the recognition demanded stems from a familiarity with marriage as the expression of the freely chosen commitment of two people to spend the rest of their lives together. From outside these groupings, the marriage or union of two people of the same sex is seen as profoundly unfamiliar. I say "profoundly" only to capture the marked sense of discomfort exhibited by some, leading them to declare such unions "unnatural," thus contrasting it with a sense of the natural as something more comfortably experienced as "the way things are" and, presumably, were meant to be. However, what I think needs to be pointed out is that the articulated demand to have same-sex unions recognized as marriages is one that is based on a context of familiarity with the concept of marriage as a freely chosen commitment shared by two people, a concept of marriage that contrasts with, say, the concept of marriage as a union arranged for the mutual benefit of two families.

When this concept is stressed one can see how the unfamiliarity that some people have with the practice of two people of the same sex making such a commitment is not a radical unfamiliarity but one that *qualifies* this more basic familiarity with the practice of freely choosing one's spouse, as opposed, again, to a practice where the choice is made by someone else. It is on this basis that there is, for everyone involved—those who support same-sex marriages as well as those who oppose them—an implicit recognition of their existence, indeed of their coexistence with other forms of union within the wider network of social relationships that make up the social world. What the demand for recognition does is render explicit this heretofore implicit recognition, which has the effect of challenging the familiar ways we have for rendering and accounting for the terms of our coexistence. In other words, this articulated demand for recognition reveals a situation that calls for "*re*-cognition," a rethinking of the ways in which we relate to each other. This, I believe, is why it is important to attend carefully to demands for recognition. Such demands usually lay bare certain implicit features that regulate and structure the dynamics of social life—they question the predominant account of the "transfamilial narrative," as it were.

Charles Taylor has done much to help us understand the crucial role that the notion of recognition plays in the ordering and disordering of social life. In his influential essay "The Politics of Recognition," he links the demand for recognition on the part of minority groups to the notion of the very self-identity of those groups. He writes (p. 25):

> The thesis is that our identity is partly shaped by recognition or its absence, often
> by the misrecognition of others, and so a person or group of people can suffer real
> damage, real distortion, if the people or society around them mirror back to them a
> confining or demeaning or contemptible picture of themselves. Non-recognition or
> misrecognition can inflict harm, can be a form of oppression, imprisoning someone
> in a false, distorted, and reduced mode of being.

To put this in terms of the dynamics of social life as I have been describing them here, non-recognition and misrecognition have both implicit and explicit dimensions. Implicit non-recognition or misrecognition can, and often does, lead to demands for recognition. Such demands have the effect, if they are sufficiently persistent, of rendering explicit those implicit forms of non-recognition or misrecognition. Such explicit non-recognition or misrecognition can of course, as Taylor points out, inflict harm and be oppressive to those demanding recognition. However, if we want to move beyond this situation, we need to move beyond the dynamics of simple recognition, or lack of it, and engage a process of "*re*-cognition," or, in Russon's term, of "self-transcending critique," rethinking the situation in light of the demands being expressed and their graded levels of acceptance or rejection.

It is not enough simply to accept or reject a demand for recognition. To remain at this level signals a failure to engage a new situation, a situation that cannot, can no longer, be fully recognized along familiar lines, neither along those that generate the demand, nor along those that the demand addresses. At the heart of demands for recognition one can discern a questioning of the conditions of coexistence that sustain different ways of life, different ways of making sense of the world. It is this questioning that needs to be addressed and it requires us to rethink those conditions of coexistence that sustain everyone involved. This rethinking involves the effort to move beyond, without abandoning, one's familiarities and to engage this same effort issuing from another set of familiarities.

In other words, simple coexistence must rearticulate common ground. This is difficult work, largely because it is initially disoriented and disorienting, and there is a great temptation to retreat into one's familiarities, rather than question them in light of the demands being made, or to reduce those demands to terms that do not question those familiarities, that do not pose the problem and challenge of rearticulation. For example, in the assertion that same-sex unions cannot be considered marriages, because marriage means the union of a man and a woman for the purpose of procreation, so such unions will just have to be considered something else, there is no attempt to rearticulate common ground. There is merely an attempt to return to simple coexistence along previously familiar lines, ignoring the changed conditions that the demand has created.

What seems to me to be important about this account is that it helps to see how the failure to engage in critical self-transcendence is not merely a lack, but is in fact a *retreat* from reality, a retreat into one's familiarities, in a way that can only exacerbate the sense of surrounding unfamiliarities. We cannot escape from the social dynamics that structure and challenge social life, any more than we can ultimately escape from reality. A social dynamic that promotes certain familiarities over others is one characterized by the retreat of some from real contact with others—the example of the creation of gated communities comes to mind—and cannot be said truly to respond to actual conditions.

John Russon provides us with a very rich conceptual framework for making sense of our social dynamic, which recognizes that we are grounded in the concrete familiarities of lived experience, but that this groundedness is structurally open to the unfamiliarity that contact with a developing world invariably reveals. Indeed, his account allows him to formulate what in fact can be explicitly articulated as the telos of social life. If, as he writes, we are to understand the human condition or human life as necessarily "structured by specially figured social familiarities," then, as he puts it in *Human Experience* (p. 72), "the society that is universally open to the human condition must be one that accepts this necessity of social diversity as its premise."

Note, however, that Russon says "premise," not "conclusion." Social diversity merely describes the various familiarities that human beings have established in making sense of the world. These familiarities also establish a contact with the world that is, essentially, openness to it. In Russon's words:

> The givenness of this variety, though the starting point for intersubjectivity, is not the finished state of human contact . . . [The] universal human condition is to be a plural situation of cultural narratives, each of which is inherently propelled towards transcending and transforming these given differences through establishing a communication between them.

Thus, for Russon, transcendence is transformation, and our openness to and within human contact is a transformation of the given into a richer sense of reality.

Russon (p. 69) further articulates the two poles that frame his understanding of the organization of social life, in which "the move from family life to social life can take forms that approximate more to the particularism of the family or more to the universalism of cosmopolitan life." He goes on to write (p. 72) that it is this "cosmopolitan extreme that marks the most fully fledged social structure," for the simple reason that it shows us "the *terminus ad quem* of the development of human self-identity," in the sense that it reveals "the form of the inherent goal of the human project of mutual, equal recognition." It should be pointed out that Russon is here discussing the *form* of the inherent goal of mutual, equal recognition, and his account shows how the *substance* of such recognition has yet to be fully played out.

In order to grasp the substance of this working out of the telos of mutual recognition we need to follow the dynamic interaction of the familiar and the unfamiliar. That is, we can see how the cosmopolitan ideal is actually at work in contemporary attempts to create the conditions for multicultural coexistence. The importance of looking to the multicultural, rather than merely postulating the ideal, is that it illustrates, graphically and plainly, the dynamic of the familiar and the unfamiliar. Indeed, it can be said to embody this dynamic, in the sense that it explicitly recognizes how familiarity figures one's sense of oneself, while at the same time it explicitly recognizes that one's contact with others demands that one negotiate that familiarity.

In other words, I am suggesting that multicultural societies embody at the level of lived experience the dynamic that Russon describes, complete with the telos of mutual, equal recognition, which does not appeal to the abstract universality that renders the cosmopolitan ideal so problematic. In addition, however, the struggles within multicultural societies also reveal the ways in which this telos is occulted, precisely because of the failure to engage the process of self-transcending critique that Russon identifies, the failure to test one's familiarities against reality. Too often, our multicultural reality is interpreted, not in terms of both the telos and the dynamics that it exhibits, but strictly in terms of familiar narratives, whether explicitly, in terms of a dominant culture's values and traditions, or implicitly, by appealing to a framework that claims to be neutral but is in fact the familiar cultural narrative of universal humanity, which assumes that the common ground of coexistence always already exists, either beneath our differences, within a shared human nature, or above them, as a regulative ideal, that is, something that we strive for while knowing that its achievement will never be fully realized. In either case there is a refusal to engage in self-transcending critique, a refusal to see that actually engaging the demands of the world is, in effect, to participate in changing it. This multicultural reality I refer to is not an ideal, nor a given, but a social configuration that embodies the dynamic of the familiar and unfamiliar in a way that enables us to see more clearly the telos of mutual, equal recognition. To see it is to enact it, as in the therapy and pedagogy described by Russon (p. 141): "simply the self-conscious taking up of this project of recognition, such that one pursues being recognized through facilitating the recognizing of others."

To reformulate all of this in the terms of the speculative philosophy of history I have introduced, what Russon offers us—and in this he can be said to be following Hegel—is a reformulated telos that arises out of the actual dynamics of history. That is, the telos of mutual, equal recognition through mutual education and communication arises out of the dynamics of human development, as these manifest themselves in the self-consciousness provoked by the self-transcending critique of the limits of familial social relations, themselves provoked by the encounter with unfamiliarities, and, even more explicitly in an increasingly multicultural world, of the daily encounter of unfamiliar familiarities. If this sounds too smooth, it is because the whole process is being described at a very high level of generality, which, again, is the task that philosophy sets itself.

However, one need only think of the dynamics of one's own family life to see how the process is anything but smooth. Yet if the dynamics of family life are not smooth, it is because, as Russon argues, the recognition afforded within families is largely implicit and, because it is implicit, is left unquestioned and/or taken for granted. These "family narratives" are, in a sense, basic—they give each of us our original orientation to the world—but that orientation is not a self-conscious one until it encounters a reality that challenges it.

There is a marvellous expression in French: "*petits enfants, petits soucis; grands enfants, grands soucis*" ("small children, small worries; big children, big worries"). The realities that children encounter, say, at school, shake up their confidence in the world, effectively disorienting them, but they return (hopefully) to family lives that, through the unquestioning support and comfort they provide, mitigate the effects of that disorientation and, through the unquestioned familial narrative they provide, permit the children to reorient themselves when returning to school with, in Russon's terms, their sense of "I-can" suitably reinforced. Thus the "small worries" that traverse their relatively restricted lives are not debilitating. Part of the difficulty of being a "big child" —an adult— with an adult's worries is that the unquestioning support and comfort provided by one's family, and the unquestioned familial narrative it provides, play much smaller roles in defining how one is called upon to orient oneself within, and respond to, one's encounter with extrafamilial others. Adulthood requires self-consciousness, which itself requires a critical ability to question oneself in one's relation to others, such that mutual recognition is achieved.

Again, as Russon points out, to step outside the unquestioned familial narrative into a social space traversed and structured by extrafamilial narratives is not to step out of one world and into another. It is, in fact, to become increasingly self-conscious about the social space one orients oneself within, which includes recognizing—indeed, is largely defined through the recognition of—others who themselves of course presuppose particular narratives. The typical story we tell ourselves of this process—call it the story of "socialization"—is that family life prepares its members for functional roles within the wider society, where they are called upon to "make a living." Is this typical story we tell ourselves adequate to an increasingly multicultural world?

Let us look again at how Russon describes the logic of the dynamics of social life, and then we will contrast it with the concern raised by Kymlicka with regard to the limits to relying on what Kymlicka calls "mutual understanding" for guaranteeing "social stability." Russon writes (p. 69):

> Typically, one is not born into a family simply, but into a family within an already
> determinate social environment, and the narrative the family enforces through its
> behavior will have to find a way to reconcile itself with the larger narratives enforced
> by the society as a whole, just as the narratives of individual family members must fit
> into the narrative of the overall family power structure if the individuals (the family
> in the former case, the family members in the latter) are to be able to function. The
> family is thus both an autonomous form of intersubjective experience and also an

agent for initiating the family members into the larger form of social experience. It certainly is true that there can be families that do not function well, and it certainly is true that there can be societies with sufficient complexity or looseness of definition that the precise familial narrative is very far removed from the precise social narrative, but *it still must be the case that there be some ground of reconciliation* [my emphasis] of the family and the larger society if the family is to be able to function within that society that contextualizes it. While there can be extreme variation, then, the logic behind the structure of the family and its relation to society means that it is normally the case that the narrative enacted within familial behavior equally serves to reproduce the larger social narrative.

Many people, typically those who are worried about where we are headed within our increasingly multicultural world, might be wondering to what extent this logic still holds. It is the continued viability of this logic that clearly worries Kymlicka. One might describe his effort to make sense of our increasingly multicultural world in terms of granting a form of recognition to minorities that possess a "societal culture" and ensuring the fair integration of individuals who do not, or rather have left their societal culture behind, as a way of defending the viability of the logic described above. Minorities possessing societal cultures are granted minority rights that allow them to distinguish themselves from the majority culture because they respect the dynamics of the social logic that allows familial behaviour to "reproduce the larger social narrative," at least as far as the latter is embodied in the basic institutions that support the modern state form. It is for the same reason that particular immigrating individuals and their families should expect, not the specific minority rights afforded to societal cultures, but fair terms of integration into the larger social narrative that they have chosen to join through immigration.

If Kymlicka seems to accept the basic logic that Russon identifies, one might say that he would define present multicultural societies as in fact displaying a situation where familial narratives can in fact, as Russon allows, be quite "far removed" from the predominant social narrative. This distance is encapsulated in Kymlicka's use (again, in his paper "Multicultural States and Intercultural Citizens") of the idea of "pluralism," which, in this context and using Russon's terminology, might be understood as a convenient way to express the varying distances that exist between familial and social narratives, such that one cannot rely on any smooth transition from one to the other. Indeed, it is precisely because such smooth transitions are lacking that Kymlicka downplays the significance of developing what he calls "intercultural citizenship," because of the tensions that animate the relations between cultures. Kymlicka argues (p. 166) that when one considers what he calls intercultural citizenship and multicultural justice:

three possible areas of tension have been raised between the two: (1) that the intercultural citizen may prefer global interculturalism, while multicultural justice requires focusing on local interculturalism; (2) that the model of the intercultural citizen requires a level of intercultural exchange which may unfairly burden some isolationist groups; and (3) that the model of the intercultural citizen requires a level of mutual understanding that is either tokenistic (if focused on superficial cultural differences) or utopian (if focused on deep cultural differences), while justice requires acknowledging the limits of mutual understanding and accepting the partial opaqueness of our differences.

Kymlicka seeks to promote the principles of justice that will afford a more stable social context within which the transition from familial to social narratives can take place. As long as the state form guarantees the basic rights of all and does not forcibly assimilate or exclude duly recognized members of a given multicultural society, which of course is the social narrative that Kymlicka contributes to, then sufficient space can be given to various familial narratives as long as they do not undermine the larger social narrative.

However, part of the point of Russon's account is that the larger social narrative itself grows out of and develops from the familial narratives. This is why Russon insists that "it still must be the case that there be some ground of reconciliation of the family and the larger society if the family is to able to function within that society that contextualizes it." For Russon, as for Hegel, that ground of reconciliation is to be found in the process of recognizing one another. Remember that the recognition afforded by families is implicit and (largely) unquestioned. In contrast, the recognition required and afforded by social life itself needs to be explicit and a function of the "self-transcending critique" of those self-conscious efforts that render such recognition explicit. It is this movement of rendering explicit what is lived implicitly within the familial/familiar narratives that links the dynamics of coexistence to the telos of mutual, equal self-conscious recognition. It is because Kymlicka understands the dynamics of coexistence much as Kant does, as largely conflictual or "unsocial," that he turns our attention away from them in order to focus on the telos which, again as with Kant, concerns principles of justice that can be placed above conflicts in order to mediate them. It is in the name of such principles that Kymlicka downplays the fruits to be born of "mutuality," which he otherwise considers to be admirable. He believes that what he calls "mutual understanding" too easily becomes "either tokenistic (if focused on superficial cultural differences) or utopian (if focused on deep cultural differences), while justice requires acknowledging the limits of mutual understanding and accepting the partial opaqueness of our differences." In urging us to acknowledge the "limits of mutual understanding," Kymlicka is in fact betraying the social logic described above by refusing to see within his telos of justice the dynamics of social life. Now, however, we are in a position to ask: if the telos of justice does not arise out of the dynamics of social life, where does it come from?

In order to answer this, I think it is important to point out the fundamental difference between the conception of "mutual understanding," as Kymlicka describes it, and the "mutual recognition" that Russon identifies as the *terminus ad quem* of social life. Kymlicka does not believe that any kind of "deep mutual understanding" should be the basis for ensuring a stable social order, given the pluralistic conditions of contemporary societies, or put more simply, given our increasingly multicultural world. If Kymlicka is concerned with ensuring a stable social order within contemporary pluralistic conditions, it is because he sees within those conditions considerable unrest and instability. What if what he deems to be factors of "instability" are merely certain consequences emanating from the way in which the dynamics of social life are manifested within those current conditions? What if the concern for "instability" is one that arises more out of the attempt to stand outside the actual dynamics of (historical) social life in order the "better" to judge it from the perspective of its ultimate telos, Kant's "cosmopolitan point of view"? What happens if we try instead to view the contemporary "pluralistic" conditions of social life from the perspective of their telos as emanating from their dynamics?

Arguably, this is what Russon is attempting to do by identifying the *terminus ad quem* of social life as "mutual, equal recognition." Such a notion captures not only the telos of social life, it also describes its dynamics. For Russon, social life both *aims* at mutual, equal recognition and *is driven* or animated by the actual process of recognizing others through contact. This is what Russon calls "the human condition." The human condition contains within its development or unfolding the conditions of a "universal" society, which we need to understand as (Russon, p. 72) "creating itself as networks of self-transcending intersubjective contacts from out of specifically figured situations of social familiarity." This is how we need to understand our "pluralistic" conditions, not as conditions harbouring the potential for ceaseless conflicts that need to be mitigated and mediated by principles that somehow can be articulated as transcending those conflicts, but as generating the real possibility of genuine recognition of actual differences within a developing social whole, what Étienne Balibar would call "ideal universality." Russon writes (p. 72):

> The "universal" society, then, is one that acknowledges the experiential primacy of cultural pluralism—of narrative pluralism—and sees the universality of any shared human environment as something to be achieved through learning to make such narratives communicate, rather than as a given, already existent situation of human equality. The human condition is this given variety of narrative differences.

> The givenness of this variety, though the starting point for intersubjectivity, is not the finished state of human contact, for it is itself—like the body and like the family—a self-transcending situation of openness, in that . . . the goal of achieving this universality is inherent to the form of every social narrative qua social narrative. *The universal human condition is to be a plural situation of cultural narratives, each of which is inherently propelled toward transcending and transforming these given differences through establishing a communication between them* [my emphasis].

One should read this last sentence as giving us a fuller sense of what we mean—or should be made to realize we mean—when we say that that the world is "increasingly becoming multicultural." The world increasingly recognizes that "the plural situation of cultural narratives" describes the context within which we need to understand and make sense of the contact between people. Rather than see this as a conflict-ridden situation that must be mitigated if we are to avoid what are deemed to be disastrous consequences, the contact of these narratives propels them towards an identification and ultimate reconciliation of differences, precisely because that contact establishes and maintains communication between those differences. The point is not to deny the presence of conflict, but to contextualize conflicts within the dynamics within which they take place.

I can picture many people shaking their heads here, because they are incredulous. Perhaps, however, their incredulity is less a function of the incredible nature of what is being said than a consequence of being asked to consider such a carefully worked-out speculative framework. Perhaps there are people who are shaking their heads because they are thinking of the "facts of the matter." For them, the conflicts that one finds throughout this increasingly multicultural world speak for themselves. Yet of course they do not. Neither the facts, nor the conflicts, speak for themselves. *We* do that, *we* speak through and with them. What the speculative effort is all about is providing a wider framework within which we can speak about them, and through and with them. Remember that speculative philosophy does not deny facts. Like everyone else, it appeals to them, but not to this other, no less speculative but insufficiently philosophical idea that facts "speak for themselves."

What we might ask of Russon's speculative framework, however, is how it fits, or how it should be articulated, within the speculative framework of the past-present-future complex. That is, although Russon does allow us to talk about both the dynamics and the telos of social life, what happens when we ask how social life itself is articulated with history, understood speculatively as the past-present-future complex? I think this is an important question because Russon has done us an invaluable service in showing how this project of recognition is at the heart of individual or familial development. At the heart of this development there is a social dynamic at work. However, part of the force of Russon's argument is that, because the focus is on individual self-development, understood within its wider familial and social context, it can rely on the experience of maturation that each of goes through more or less successfully. Indeed, Russon gives us a reading of that process that is both profound and far-reaching. However, what is still missing is a more fully developed account of the development of the social dynamic itself, which, I would argue, cannot rely on the experience of maturation, but must instead pay particular attention to wider historical considerations. In other words, what is required is a more fully fledged development of the philosophy of history that underpins the telos, the *terminus ad quem*, that Russon has helped us identify within our individual efforts to make sense of our lives. To do that we shall turn to Hegel's speculative philosophy of history.

4

Hegel, the Particularity of Conflicts, and the Spaces of "Reason-ability"

A fully fledged philosophy of history can be found in the work of Hegel, a key inspiration for John Russon's account, as well as for the more general account, of the importance of the role and function of *recognition* for understanding the dynamics of social life, as well as its overall direction. I have already cited Charles Taylor's use of this theme of recognition and, more importantly, of the possibility of *mis*recognition, in speaking of the question of our identities. In the same essay, "The Politics of Recognition," Taylor claims (pp. 25–26) that:

> our identity is partly shaped by recognition or its absence, often by the
> misrecognition of others, and so a person or group of people can suffer real damage,
> real distortion, if the people or society around them mirror back to them a confining
> or demeaning or contemptible picture of themselves. . . . misrecognition shows not
> just a lack of due respect. It can inflict a grievous wound, saddling its victims with
> a crippling self-hatred. Due recognition is not just a courtesy we owe people. It is a
> vital human need.

I would like to temper Taylor's discussion in order to enable us to move beyond this particular mode of insistence, not because I do not think that what Taylor describes is true—misrecognition certainly can have devastating effects in any given case—but because of the particular role that recognition has in the *composition* or *constitution* of social life. Recognition needs to be seen as structuring the *dynamics* of social life. That is, *mis*recognition points to a social life whose dynamics are more or less dysfunctional. Russon's discussion allows us to see that quite clearly. If the implicit recognition afforded to members of particular families stifles or distorts the sense of "I-can" that families are meant to provide, then one can expect significant problems in the dynamics of the wider social life. I ask anyone now merely to think about the dynamics of their workplace to get an idea of what is being pointed to here.

Non-recognition, however, is quite different from misrecognition, in the sense that, if the latter can be said to disturb or disarrange the dynamics of social life, the former can be said to disrupt them. Thus, to recall Alain Touraine's discussion, it is non-recognition that increasingly characterizes the "demodernizing" process at work in contemporary societies, where people increasingly interact economically and instrumentally, but retreat from interaction when it becomes a question of values, meaning, and significance. That is, the social dynamic of recognition is restricted to instrumental terms in the wider economic sphere, and its interpersonal and affective functions are split off from that wider sphere into increasingly isolated pockets of significance.

Another way of putting this is to suggest that, rather than point to the function of recognition the way Taylor does by calling it a "vital human need," we would do better to consider it in terms of its function in a vital human dynamic, the relational structure of human interaction. Recognition threads together the social whole and fuels its overall functioning. Because it does so, the fabric of social life can be stretched and even torn when that recognition is dysfunctional. Similarly, the dynamics of social life can sputter and stall when that fuel is lacking.

If we push this analogy of recognition as fuelling the dynamics of social life a little further, we can begin to respond to the question of how and why the dynamics of social life should be understood within the wider dynamics of the historical life of human beings considered as a whole, or what is called speculative philosophy of history, the past-present-future complex within which our lives unfold. We have seen through our discussion of Russon that our lives do not merely mechanically unfold, each day giving way to the next, but rather take place within a particular narrative, "which is inherently propelled toward transcending and transforming" the given differences with other narratives "through establishing a communication between them." We have also seen that that which establishes this "communication" is the process of recognition, which includes its dysfunctional forms of misrecognition and non-recognition. What are we to make, however, of this idea that this whole process is "inherently propelled"? What kind of speculative move is being made here?

I have already mentioned that, if we focus on the individual's development within his or her familial and social context, then the experience of maturation itself—literally, of growing up—can plausibly be interpreted as a process that "inherently propels" our development as human beings. Is it just as plausible to

MULTICULTURAL DYNAMICS AND THE ENDS OF HISTORY

extend this experience of being "inherently propelled" to the historical process considered as a whole? The plausibility of such an idea is indeed what Hegel's speculative philosophy of history was intended to demonstrate. Hegel does so by describing the historical process as a whole as *the realization of reason*. (What follows has been developed in my "Realizing Reason in History: How Cunning Does It Have To Be?")

One might understand the connection between the realization of reason and the historical process in two ways. First, one might want to show how reason has developed and "realized itself" within history. There is reason in history, and the task of the philosopher is to show that development. Hegel indeed wishes to do precisely that. In fact, that is the title given to the *Introduction* to his *Lectures on the Philosophy of World History*. However, one can also see the relation between reason and history as much more intimate than merely one in which reason develops itself over time, as it were. One might suggest that, not only does history show us that reason has developed over time, but the task of history is precisely to develop or realize reason in and through time. There is reason in history because that is what history brings about. Thus, the "realization" of reason in history is both something that is recognized and something that must be done. For Hegel this "realization" is accomplished through the doings and sufferings of concrete human beings in their attempts to live out their lives.

Hegel wants to show that history is not a cold, anonymous process that simply sweeps up human lives and never looks back. Indeed, his philosophy of history is primarily concerned with the concrete doings and sufferings of human beings, insofar as *they* are what embody the process of reason's realization. Now, we must note that philosophy is what can show this to us because philosophy is the self-conscious appropriation of the whole process understood as a whole. This is why philosophy is, and must be understood as, speculative thought. That is, philosophy, when it contemplates history, does not despair of it—Hegel is here following Kant. As we shall see, for Hegel the true story of history is the progressive realization of reason and freedom, which both express the Idea of history. Nevertheless, Hegel recognizes (p. 68) that:

> An initial survey of history, however, would indicate that the actions of men are
> governed by their needs, passions, and interests, by the attitudes and aims to which
> they give rise, and by their own character and abilities; we gain the impression that,
> in this scene of activity, these needs, passions, interests, etc., are the sole motive
> forces. . . . When we contemplate this display of passions, and consider the historical
> consequences of their violence and of the irrationality which is associated with them
> (and even more so with good intentions and worthy aims); when we see the evil,
> the wickedness, and the downfall of the most flourishing empires the human spirit
> has created; and when we are moved to profound pity for the untold miseries of

individual human beings—we can only end with a feeling of sadness at the transience of everything.

However, we should not let such a feeling of sadness take over our thinking about this process of history. Indeed, Hegel warns (p. 69) against those who, becoming defeatist about the overall movement of history, "retreat into that selfish complacency which stands on the calmer shore and, from a secure position, smugly looks on at the distant spectacle of confusion and wreckage.". Hegel asks us what is to be thought when contemplating the spectacle of history:

> But even as we look upon history as an altar on which the happiness of nations,
> the wisdom of states, and the virtue of individuals are slaughtered, our thoughts
> inevitably impel us to ask: to *whom*, or to what *ultimate end*, have these monstrous
> sacrifices been made?

In asking this question thought is making the distinction between the *means* of history and the *end* of history, another way of expressing what I have been calling the *dynamics* of history and the *telos* of history. It is this distinction that will allow us to get beyond the dismal spectacle of what Kant called "the idiotic course of things human." A good part of Hegel's *Introduction* is devoted to working out this distinction.

Hegel begins by discussing what he calls the "general concept" of a philosophical appreciation of history, or what is now called speculative philosophy of history. He notices right off (p. 27) that "the main objection levelled at philosophy is that it imports its own thoughts into history and considers the latter in the light of the former."

However, it is not so much that philosophy imports its own thoughts into history, since, after all, philosophy, or philosophizing, takes place within history. Rather, it looks at history from a philosophical perspective. Essentially, what this means for Hegel is that "the only thought which philosophy brings with it is the simple idea of reason—the idea that reason governs the world, and that world history is therefore a rational process." He elaborates (p. 28):

> We must bring to history the belief and conviction that the realm of the will is not
> at the mercy of contingency. That world history is governed by an ultimate design,
> that it is a rational process—whose rationality is not that of a particular subject, but
> a divine and absolute reason—this is a proposition whose truth we must assume; its
> proof lies in the study of world history itself, which is the image and enactment of
> reason.

When we read this passage we need to remember that Hegel was lecturing in 1830, and could refer to a "divine and absolute reason" with relatively little comment. The point that needs to be emphasized in the context of this discussion is the idea that the "realm of the will," that is, our lives as they unfold, should not be understood to be at the mercy of contingency. This is not to say that they do not have contingent features, such as the birth and death of each one of us. Indeed, in terms of the modal square, the contingency at the heart of our lives describes our present within the past-present-future complex. Not to be at its mercy is not to isolate that present from the past and the future to which it belongs. This is the philosophical idea that is being brought to our consideration of history.

Hegel also expresses his idea in the following sentence (p. 29): "Whoever looks at the world rationally will find that it in turn assumes a rational aspect; the two exist in a reciprocal relationship." It is important to note here that Hegel does *not* say that the world as a whole has to be considered rational. Reason does not take up the whole of the world, it leaves behind the merely contingent, understood here, not in terms of the modal square, but, for example, with reference to such contingencies as my skin colour, or my receding hairline, or the size of my feet. The point to be developed is the idea of *reciprocity* between the rational dealing with the world and a world that responds in kind by displaying itself as rational.

This is how those who would focus on history as conflict can be shown to be mistaken. It is not that they are wrong to point to the various conflicts that traverse history. Nor are they wrong to insist on trying to come to terms with such conflict, or to regard it as a cause for concern. On the contrary, Hegel would agree that the *appearance* of conflict within history is what calls for our considered attention. However, a philosophical history cannot remain at the level of contemplating such conflict, nor should it pretend to offer "solutions" to the "problems" that such conflict, considered in this abstract fashion, poses. Rather, its point is to show how, within the appearance of conflict, reason is actually working itself out.

After the explication of the general concept, the next division in Hegel's *Introduction* is "The Realization of Spirit in History." This division is itself subdivided into four sections: "The Determination of Spirit," "The Means of its Realization," "The Material of its Realization," and "Its Reality." What Hegel does in these sections, to state it succinctly, is to argue that the "determination of spirit" is the freedom at the heart of human efforts to realize what human beings find within themselves to realize. It is a freedom precisely because their efforts depend only on themselves, and not on something like animal instincts. The means of this realization are the passions and interests that animate the particular lives of human beings. Its material is the social organization of those passions and interests into a developing whole, which Hegel calls the "state." Its reality is the actually existing dynamics of the historical life of these developing wholes.

I cannot here go into the details of Hegel's account. My focus is on understanding what it means, and what it involves, to think of reason as actually working itself out within the conflicts of history. First of all, we need to ask if there is a general way in which we can define the conflict that history displays. That is, is there a general way to explain why there is such conflict in history? A fairly traditional way of doing so is to say that the conflicts of history arise out of, and are fuelled by, the passions of human beings. Human beings tend to get "carried away" in the things that they do when these are accompanied by strong beliefs and commitments. Of course, human beings also cannot do without these strong beliefs and commitments, for they are what human beings are animated by, making of them the particular engaged human beings that they are. (Human beings who are lacking in passion are lacking in engagement in the world. They are listless, passive, conformist, but, interestingly, just as prone to passionate outbursts as anyone else. Whether or not such outbursts can find channels of productive engagement, or merely spend themselves without being engaged in anything other than their own display, might be considered the principal question of education. But such a discussion will have to wait for another time.) In fact, this insistence on the passionate nature of human beings not only explains the prevalence of conflict within history, it can, in the context of our discussion of where we are headed in an increasingly multicultural world, be given an even more speculative twist that can serve as a contrast to Hegel's (and my) own.

The late Stuart Hampshire argued in his book *Justice is Conflict* that the presence of conflict in human affairs is ineliminable, and needs to be thought as actually providing for the conditions of human justice. To put part of his argument in my terms, Hampshire is saying that conflict is not an affront to the telos of justice but, on the contrary, is the arena within which the dynamics of human interaction can produce justice, by mediating conflicts in ways that make life livable. Conflict arises out of human interaction because human beings are diverse. Human beings are diverse because their experiences, as these are shaped by their memories and imaginations, are diverse. More forcefully, Hampshire says (pp. 37–38):

> the diversity and divisiveness of languages and of cultures and of local loyalties is not a superficial but an essential and deep feature of human nature—both unavoidable and desirable—and rooted in our divergent imaginations and memories. More fundamentally, our stronger sentiments are exclusive and immediately lead to competition and conflict, because our memories, and with them our imagination,

are focused upon particular persons, particular inherited languages, particular places, particular social groups, particular rituals and religions, and particular tones of voice; and hence our stronger loyalties are similarly focused. We want to serve and to reinforce the particular institutions that protect us, and to extend their power and influence at the expense of their rivals.

One might describe what Hampshire is pointing to and arguing for here as the *primacy of familiarity*. Each of us is passionately rooted in a particular and familiar world that we are committed to defending against the unfamiliarities of worlds that conflict with it. Hampshire pursues this speculative line of thinking, fully recognizing its speculative character, as follows (pp. 38–39):

> Men and women are naturally driven to resist any external force that tends to repress their typical activities or to limit their freedom. This is true of individuals, families, social classes, religious groups, ethnic groups, nations. This is the common order of nature. They are all, these different units, struggling, wittingly or unwittingly, to preserve their individual character and their distinctive qualities against the encroachment and absorption of other self-assertive things in their environment... It is a natural necessity for each distinct entity to try to preserve its distinctiveness for as long as it can, and for this reason conflicts are at all times to be expected in the history of individuals, of social groups, and of nations, as their paths intersect. There is no end to conflict within and around the civil order.

Now, presumably, in an increasingly multicultural world such "paths" can be expected increasingly to "intersect," and thus more and more conflicts can be expected as well. This is where Hampshire's notion of justice arises. Because of the increased intersection of familiarities and the conflicts they create, there arises an increased sense of the need to mediate such conflicts, in order to avoid mutual destructiveness, and to organize relevant institutions that can ensure the "negotiations" and "arbitrations" that will settle given menacing disputes, without arguing for, or even hoping for, the elimination of all conflict, insofar as the latter remains grounded in forms of social familiarity. Indeed, it is in recognition of that grounded familiarity that Hampshire argues (p. 40), first, "that bringing into existence institutions and recognized procedures should have priority over declarations of universal principles"; and, second, "that institutions earn respect mainly from their customary use and from gradually acquired familiarity." The hope and the expectation are, then, that what will arise out of this process is:

> a rough sense of fairness in the adjudication of conflicts, always given equality of access: not perfect fairness, but the kind of imperfect fairness that may emerge from

procedures which are themselves compromises, from the relics of history. Nothing more is reasonably to be expected.

This all seems very reasonable, and that, of course, is the point. Like most forms of "reasonableness," Hampshire's is sceptical about the powers of human reason. Specifically, it is sceptical about the powers of human reason in the face of the powers of human passions. Hampshire should not, of course, be read as in any way denigrating human rationality or the articulation of principles. He merely wishes to contextualize such articulations within their actual conditions of emergence, in the dynamics of conflicting memories and imagination as these define social familiarities.

Near the end of *Justice is Conflict* Hampshire writes (p. 94): "Rationality is a bond between persons, but it is not a very powerful bond, and it is apt to fail as a bond when there are strong passions on two sides of a conflict." His "solution" to the problems generated by such situations is to promote those institutions and practices that are set up to hear the different sides of a particular dispute with a view to resolving it, not to the satisfaction of everyone involved, but in a way that all sides can agree is fair. In other words, for Hampshire the telos of justice needs to be subordinated to the dynamics of social life, rather than have those same dynamics subordinate themselves to justice articulated as a telos towards which social life is deemed to be ultimately directed. Hampshire himself says that in this he is merely recognizing the wisdom of the famous dictum of David Hume: "Reason is, and ought to be, the slave of the passions." Interestingly, I suppose because of the philosopher's commitment to rationality, Hampshire feels compelled to add (pp. xii–xiii):

> It is difficult to acknowledge the bare contingency of personal feeling as the final stopping point when one is arguing with oneself, or with others, about the ultimate requirements of justice. But I am now fairly sure that this is the true stopping point.

Now, the point I wish to make is this. If it is true that, at least as far as moral and political philosophy is concerned, we must accept the "bare contingency of personal feeling as the final stopping point," then moral and political philosophy—understood as arguments concerning the "ultimate requirements of justice," or the telos of social life—needs to be contextualized within speculative philosophy of history. It is precisely that "bare contingency" that we are that it seeks to make sense of by placing it in the wider movement of history, or, in the terms of the modal square, that "bare contingency" of any given present, recognizing the necessities of the past, and exploring the possibilities of the future. Only in this way can we see how any telos that we might articulate can begin to play a directive role within the dynamics that otherwise characterize our social lives.

Hegel recognizes that the passions of human beings are the driving force of history and that, taken in themselves, such passions describe the bare contingency of human life. However, like Kant, he is both amazed and horrified by what human beings have accomplished through history. If one focuses on their rational accomplishments, then one cannot rest content with describing human life strictly in terms of its bare contingency. The question that speculative philosophy of history poses is how we are to reconcile the rational accomplishments of human beings with the bare contingency of their existence. Hegel recognizes, just as Hume and Hampshire do, that our passions can and will overwhelm our "reason-ability," our ability to have reason mediate our differences and difficulties, in any given contingent situation if one takes the point of view *from* that given contingent situation. That is, any given human situation is driven by the human passions that are the dynamic forces that bind it as a particular, given situation. Such situations will be conflictual to the extent that the passions involved stem from differently developed familiarities. (Such situations can be both creatively or destructively conflictual, but more of that in a moment.) However, when we look, not at a given conflictual contingent situation, but at the process by which these conflictual situations resolve themselves through time, we notice that they display not only the spectacle of spent passions, dismally enough, but also the development and deployment of what Hegel calls "reason," and which we can call the "reason-ability" of human passions-in-situation. I make use of this notion of "reason-ability" in order to emphasize the fact that, for Hegel, reason arises out of the passionate situation of human interaction and is not something added from without. The passions are the means of its realization.

This has never been by any means a smooth process, and the evidence of destructively conflictual situations around the world suggests that it will not become so for some time. However, before inferring from this that this will always be the case, we might turn our attention to the developmental features of the process itself. In order to capture the way in which reason, when we take the long view, survives the destructiveness of human passions as they have unleashed themselves throughout history, Hegel makes use of the expression "the cunning of reason." The most famous passage in which this expression is used, in describing the historical process considered as a whole, is the following (*Introduction*, p. 89):

> Particular interests contend with one another, and some are destroyed in the process. But it is from this very conflict and destruction of particular things that the universal

emerges, and it remains unscathed itself. For it is not the universal Idea which enters into opposition, conflict, and danger; it keeps itself in the background, untouched, and unharmed, and sends forth the particular interests of passion to fight and wear themselves out in its stead. It is what we may call the *cunning of reason* that it sets the passions to work in its service, so that the agents by which it gives itself existence must pay the penalty and suffer the loss. For the latter belong to the phenomenal world, of which part is worthless and part is of positive value. The particular is as a rule inadequate in relation to the universal, and individuals are sacrificed and abandoned as a result. The Idea pays the tribute which existence and the transient world exact, but it pays it through the passions of individuals rather than out of its own resources.

I want to comment on many things in this passage, but I shall start with the last sentence. For our purposes, we should read Idea as "reason-ability," specifically, as those socially mediated spaces that allow for human beings to realize themselves through their own efforts. "Reason-ability" arises only out of a contingent situation, the transient world, but in effect it is what perdures when that contingent situation gives way to another, other passions confronting each other in terms of their relative familiarities. While our passions drive us, as animating forces, as long as we are alive, what is accomplished by our passionate engagement in the world is the sustenance of continued "reason-ability," the ability to have reason mediate the conflicting passions that animate our lives, taken individually and taken socially. This is how we need to understand what history itself means: it is the development of human "reason-ability" over time as it encounters and responds to situations that challenge it, situations to which we give the general name of "conflict." These responses are varied and diverse. They are often institutionally expressed, though they can also be embodied in informal social and cultural practices with no explicit codes and regulations. When Hegel writes that "the universal Idea . . . keeps itself in the background, untouched, and unharmed, and sends forth the particular interests of passion to fight and wear themselves out in its stead," he is referring to the way in which contemporary forms and social spaces of "reason-ability" continue to develop through the passionate expenditure that is the living out of our lives.

Here, as always in philosophy, we are dealing with a very general description, though not an abstract one, of what takes place concretely in each of our lives (or, at least, that is what philosophy attempts to do). In order to make sense of such general philosophical statements one needs to keep one eye on what goes on concretely in one's life.

For example, if you have children, you may think about what you are doing to "raise" them, that is, think about what you are doing to enable your children to deal with the emotions they feel within the particular situations they find themselves in. If they come home crying, you do not merely begin to cry along with them. Perhaps you gather them into your arms and ask them what is wrong. Depending on how taken over they are by their passions—they may be crying so hard that they cannot speak—maybe you will hold off from asking them questions and merely soothe them, that is, allow them to regain their composure, to have the intensity of their passionate expression diminish somewhat so that questions can be asked and responses can begin to sputter forth. This can take time. The explanations may be incoherent and prone to breakdown, issuing into renewed bouts of sobbing, and your questions may need once again to turn into soothing sounds (providing an interesting speculative glimpse into the origins of language) in order again to create a space and a context for the difficult effort of forming words and uttering sentences that can be understood, an ability that your children have learned from you. This is what "reason-ability" is: a space and a context we create for ourselves in which our utterances can be formulated and understood. If we stay with my everyday example, the soothing sounds and delicate questions that you make as a parent, thus providing this space and context, stem from the development of your own "reason-ability," which, of course, is prone to being overwhelmed by your own passions. Insofar as it is not, it is because the "reason" of your "reason-ability" is successfully "keeping itself in the background, untouched and unharmed." Or, in Hegel's terms, your success is a function of your being a vehicle for "reason" in this particular situation that humanly calls for it.

We can stay with this example in order to understand Hegel's further point. Imagine an older child, an adolescent, who either storms or slinks into the house, refusing to acknowledge your presence or even her own, disappearing into her room, saying nothing at meals, refusing to join in "family activities," sometimes shouting out her evident discontent, sometimes being ominously silent about it. Soothing words and delicate questions are of no use here, insofar as these are the responses that they provoke. What is "reason-able" in this situation? It will depend on the particulars, but, whatever the strategy, it will involve cunning, skill, and dexterity in the face of complicated passions, not only those of the adolescent in question, but those of the parent who wishes to help but does not know how, and, because of this inability, this powerlessness, may be prone to frustration, anger, sadness, helplessness, angst, mockery, defiance, rage or other responses. The space of "reason-ability" that the parent-as-parent has been intent on creating and sustaining proves insufficiently stable, not only to allow the adolescent to make sense of her own despondency and confusion, but for the parent-as-a-child-himself-become-parent to readily respond to the situation in a way that will allow it to develop *from* itself the resources to resolve itself. The cunning of reason manifests itself in a widened context where the other parent, or friends and other persons, recognize the situation and, through appropriately soothing or chiding, or sympathetic, or "realistic" words, help foster "reason-ability" in the situation by widening the context, allowing more space for things to get worked out between the adolescent's confusion and concern, and the reality that makes its demands on her life.

I do not need to develop the different kinds of ways these dynamics can spin out of control. When they do, it is in the absence of "reason-ability," a "reason-ability" that has withdrawn in order to preserve itself, perhaps only to reappear, sadly, tragically, in the form of a justice system or a medical system whose purpose is to re-establish order. It is interesting to note, though I won't develop it here, that such "systematic" interventions themselves will not be fully "reason-able," even on Hegel's terms, if the solutions they provide are externally imposed on the persons in question, even when they follow from what is deemed an "understanding" of the situation. Hegel's point about the cunning of "reason-ability" is that it must emerge from the dynamics themselves. That is precisely why "cunning" is required.

My purpose in describing these everyday examples of the cunning of "reason-ability" in the name of concrete considerations has been to palliate the charge of excessively abstract and general theorizing that is often levelled against speculative philosophizing. It *is* cunning, and has to be, because the passions that need to be dealt with can easily and rapidly overwhelm its efforts, as these simple everyday examples demonstrate. Hegel seeks to extend this understanding of the cunning required of reason much further, to show how it allows us to see the development of human efforts in terms of its overall direction, a development that is not itself evident in the everyday struggles that we are involved in and that we work through to the best of our abilities.

At its most general level Hegel's notion of the "cunning of reason" bears resemblance to other general ideas that attempt to make sense of the overall development of human life as it unfolds in time, such as Providence or Fate, for example. Again, such ideas are speculative ideas, and therefore distinct from what are generally called "scientific" ideas, because they attempt to think about a whole that cannot be experienced as a whole. We are in the midst of the process we are attempting to think—to make sense of—and cannot remove ourselves from it in order to *see* it as a whole. Such ideas are called for because what we *do* experience in the world is a sense of developing within it, a sense that each of our lives is something that is unfolding, that can be made sense of. They are called for because we do not live out our lives as a mere random sequence of events, void of meaning and significance. Even if many of us are prepared to accept, at some general, cosmic level, the "ultimate" insignificance of our lives, it remains the case that this is not the way we live out our lives. Such cosmic insignificance is itself a speculative proposition that one may believe or entertain, but it is not as "reason-able" as it appears, inasmuch as it does not structure most people's "reason-able" life commitments.

For example, even in our secular and technologically inspired climate, many of my students actually believe in, or claim to commit themselves, to some notion of "providence" or "fate" as providing an overall structure to their lives, in the very general sense that they think that what happens to them "happens for a reason," or that there exists, to some extent, some kind of pattern to their lives that they are meant to enact or follow and that certain specific kinds of events await them. To be sure, some of them are appealing to an explicitly religious background, while others are no doubt indebted to Hollywood plotlines. The point is that they are, more or less, attuned to the very general sense that such notions provide to their otherwise more concrete commitments and engagements in the world. I imagine that, when their encounters with certain features of the world stir up an emotional tumult that threatens to overwhelm their normal "reason-ability," such notions play a kind of soothing function similar to the one that a parent's arms and voice once played—another example of the cunning of reason.

Note, however, how an appeal to the cunning of reason differs from an appeal to "providence" or "fate". The latter notions hand over the sense-making or sense-giving power to something beyond our own puny power to make sense of our lives. That is, if one appeals to such notions as "providence" or "fate," one effectively hands one's life over to a process that has the full or real control. To appeal to the cunning of reason is, of course, to do no such thing. Hegel refuses to hand over our lives to an overpowering source. In fact, it is the passionate forces of our lives, as these reveal themselves in our emotional dealing with the world, that is overpowering, and reason must use its cunning to counter that power.

In that sense, more than Providence and Fate, Hegel's notion of the cunning of reason most resembles Kant's notion of a "secret plan of Nature," in the sense that it is *through* our passionate engagements, which Kant sums up somewhat dryly as the "self-interest" that animates the "unsocial sociability" of human beings, that reason manifests itself. For both Kant and Hegel, human beings, insofar as they are passionately engaged in living out their own lives, are actually accomplishing the ends of a far wider project, ends that they do not immediately recognize as their own. However, there is also an important difference between Kant and Hegel here. For Kant, the ends themselves describe an ideal that is detached and serves only a regulative function in relation to the real dynamics that are to bring about that ideal. Hegel, in contrast, appeals, not to a "secret plan," but to the cunning of reason, in order to show how the ideal arises out of or emerges from the dynamics of social life, the social space of "reason-ability."

Nevertheless, like Kant, Hegel wants to show how the ideal *directs* the course of history, that is, that history needs to be understood as a directed process and not merely a succession of events that, taken together, have no ultimate significance. He does this by showing that what we discover in the space of "reason-ability," which we create for ourselves in our interactions with others, is that our own self-development is something that takes place over time and is shaped by our own progressive self-realization. This is how we need to understand his claim, which I quoted earlier, that: "Whoever looks at the world rationally will find that it in turn assumes a rational aspect; the two exist in a reciprocal relationship." The various conflicts that we encounter in our experience, our contact with the world, need to be looked at rationally, which means to see within those conflicts the space of "reason-ability" that they allow. When we do this, when we attempt to look at the world rationally, we actually create this space and, conversely, the space thus created allows us to grow and develop within it. As we grow and develop within it, the space itself expands, allowing for the continued growth of "reason-abilities," of things that we show ourselves capable of doing by showing others how we do them.

We can see here why Russon, for example, reads Hegel's understanding of history and social life as a process of mutual recognition and mutual *education*. Our development as human beings, because it takes place within a social space, does not take place automatically, as it were, or even "organically." Because it takes place within a social space, it takes place within a space of "reason-ability," a space where reason is used to direct development, through parenting or schooling, for example. Reasons are given for that direction and reasons are expected from those participating in that development. The process of recognition that we owe to each other within the social space we create for ourselves is a process of mutual education. That is, the social space that we share is the space within which we account for ourselves to each other in the development of our "reason-abilities." Thus, we learn from each other increasingly what it means to be human beings within a developing social space of "reason-ability."

Now, if I seek to relate all this back to the initial question of this book—where are we headed, given that the world is increasingly becoming multicultural?—we can imagine a Hegelian answer along the following lines. Through the process of mutual recognition and mutual education that best describes the attempt to resolve the conflicts of familiarities that animate the dynamics of social life, as long as we commit ourselves to looking at the world rationally, we are headed towards an expanding space of "reason-ability" within which we will be called upon and must be prepared to account for ourselves as others are prepared to account for themselves. This space is, of course, a conflictual space because of the different familiarities that feed into it, the multicultural here being defined as the "multiply familiar," as it were. Yet, because those different familiarities are increasingly in contact in a quotidian way, they increasingly show themselves as "unfamiliar familiarities." They are thus increasingly drawn into and increasingly draw that expanding space that calls for "reasons" to regulate and govern and mediate social relations, thus increasing the "reason-ability" of the world. The cunning of reason manifests itself in the way in which the attempt to inhabit a familiar world contributes to the expansion of a world where diverse familiarities and ways of inhabiting the world are called upon to live together within a space of mutual "like-mindedness." Thus, a Hegelian account of history shows that the telos of a social life of mutual recognition arises or emerges from the very dynamics of social life, insofar as social life creates a space of "reason-ability," thus ensuring continued human development.

Some might want to ask some basic questions at this point. Is that what history *actually* shows? Or is this Hegelian account merely the old story of historical progress that, to be sure, was inspirational for a long time, but is belied by the present state of affairs? In other words, does anyone still believe in that old story? Others might want to recognize that Hegel's account, as here presented, is not merely a recounting of this old story, but one that insists that we look to the *actual* dynamics of social life. They might accept that the world is becoming increasingly multicultural, and agree that it is within those dynamics that the telos of mutual recognition is found, and not at the end of a story of human progress. Yet they too might still want to ask some basic questions. Can such dynamics and the telos that they generate really be said to be governing the course of the world? Even if reason is cunning enough to create spaces within which we effectively recognize each other and learn from each other, are these spaces not, in fact, few and far between? Is the course of the world itself subject to forces that even the cunning of reason will simply not be able to outmanoeuvre in the long run, especially if we are asked to focus on the dynamics of such limited spaces? In other words, is the general view of Hegel's philosophy as too "idealistic"—in the common use of that word, where "idealistic" means "unrealistic"—in some sense right? Even on the most charitable reading of this speculative attempt, must we not conclude with a sigh and a "would that it were so"?

I cite such questions not because I think that they are warranted but because of the fatigue they express, a fatigue in and with the speculative effort required to try to think history as a whole as the appropriate context for making sense of our unfolding lives. As Descartes says, at the end of the first of his *Meditations on First Philosophy* (p. 17):

> this undertaking is arduous, and a certain laziness brings me back to my customary way of living. I am not unlike a prisoner who enjoyed an imaginary freedom during

his sleep, but, when he later begins to suspect that he is dreaming, fears being awakened and nonchalantly conspires with these pleasant illusions. In just the same way, I fall back of my own accord into my old opinions, and dread being awakened, lest the toilsome wakefulness which follows upon a peaceful rest must be spent thenceforward not in the light but among the inextricable shadows of the difficulties now brought forward.

Note, however, the speculative dimension of these questions: it is supposed that there *is* a course of the world that is to be deemed *real*, hence the assumed "realism" underlying the questions. That supposition can and should be fleshed out, and that is precisely what speculative philosophy of history proposes to do.

Note further that we are using speculative philosophy of history in order to respond to a specific question, which, if the reader has followed us this far, needs to be taken into account, something that the objection does not do adequately. We are trying to respond to the sense we have that we are headed somewhere and that the world is increasingly becoming multicultural. This latter affirmation of the multicultural dimension of our world suggests that the course of the world has distinct features that should be thought about in their specificity.

Having said that, there is a point underlying the questions that merits attention. It is true that there is a tension between the sense we have that we are headed somewhere and the recognition that the world is becoming increasingly multicultural, and that this tension suggests a general discomfort and unease. That is, the sense that the world as a whole is progressing toward better days is *not* as predominant as it once was, and even the idea that history manifests itself developmentally, that is, in stages, each building itself out the earlier one, is often questioned, even by historians. There is a general sense that the complexity of the world simply does not allow for the kinds of speculative moves that philosophy of history makes. The unease expressed here with speculative philosophy of history betrays a distrust of history itself, of the view that human beings are best understood in terms of various engagements over and in time. In the end, the objection seems to imply that history is not the best overall context within which to understand human beings. The past-present-future complex is simply too complex to be encapsulated within any overarching conception. Historians study the past, social and political theorists study the present, and the future cannot be studied because it is not yet and we cannot know what impact we are having on the future, nor predict how the future will deal with what we are bequeathing it.

Indeed, the twentieth century has taught us that we should temper our attempts to master the dynamics of history because such projects of mastery can lead to disastrous consequences. The spaces of "reason-ability" can feed into projects that seem far from reasonable—colonial conquest and imperial expansion, on the one hand, or ethnic reaction and other forms of retrenchment, on the other. It would be better to be wary of such grandiose schemes that seek to order the historical process in terms of either its dynamics or its telos. If we want to continue to be critical of present developments, then we should focus our attention on having them be true to the professed values and commitments that are said to animate them, and control, as best we can, the unintended and unexpected effects of what actually materializes.

In the next Part I will attempt to show that there is something to the "realistic" objection to the "idealist" pretensions of speculative philosophy of history, its attempt to understand human history as a developmental whole that focuses on the development of reason and the spaces in which it flourishes. That is, although Hegel's speculative philosophy of history is an improvement on Kant's, insofar as it provides a better account of how the telos of history can be seen to arise out of the dynamics of history, its consideration of those dynamics as structured by mutual recognition may in the end result in satisfying itself too quickly with unduly restricted spaces of developing freedom.

However, we should not let such considerations lead us to abandon our concern with the movement of history itself and the sense that it might have.

PART III

The Basic Struggle

5

Marx, Productive Forces, and History

The main purpose of this book is to ask the question stated in the introduction: given our increasingly multicultural world, where are we headed? The first Part of this book examined Kant's speculative philosophy of history, which provided a telos to history—the full development of our natural capacities within the context of a universal civic society—that could be said to respond to the question: where are we headed? The second Part of this book made use of Hegel's speculative philosophy of history principally in order to show how the dynamics of history are especially evident in our increasingly multicultural world through the development of spaces of "reason-ability," characterized by mutual recognition. In this Part I would like to combine both elements of the original question once again. In the next chapter I shall look at how Michael Hardt and Antonio Negri take up Marx's basic approach within our more explicitly multicultural context, but first, in this chapter, I shall reconsider the question of where we are headed by considering Marx's speculative philosophy of history.

Marx famously said that he stood Hegel on his head, which of course is a very awkward position for anyone to be put in. I shall not be concerned in what follows with working out that particular move on Marx's part, other than to say that, for Marx (*Selected Writings*, p. 81), Hegel "found only the *abstract, logical, speculative* expression of the movement of history, not the *actual* history of man as a given subject," and that this was insufficient. I agree with Marx here, at least in the sense that our abstract, logical, speculative expressions, which, after all, are pretty much what books in philosophy are meant to comprise, should enable us to grasp *better* "the actual history of man as a given subject." I hope to have shown that the dynamics of mutual recognition that one finds in Hegel, suitably updated by such writers as John Russon, can actually help us do precisely that, at least to some extent.

However, the forms that such recognition take can end up settling around certain kinds of formality that, if they do not betray the movement of history that gives rise to them, can often become detached from that movement. (I have not discussed it here, but this is one danger of focusing, as Hegel does, on the state as the privileged site for historical development.) As detached from the actual movement of history, such forms of recognition can become either dead weights, shouldered by some but not others, or obstacles that break or disrupt the flow of historical movement, that is, the "*actual* history of man as a given subject." To put it another way: while it is true that the dynamics of mutual recognition can and do create spaces of "reason-ability" within our passionate engagement with each other and the world, the creation of those spaces is not what best describes the "*actual* history of man as a given subject."

What, then, does better describe this "*actual* history"? Marx wants to show us that it is the productive forces that have developed out of our passionate engagements with each other and the world (of nature) that are at the heart of "*actual* history," and not "reason-ability" itself.

"Reason-ability" remains crucial and important. This book, the fact that you are reading it, and the fact that it discusses the writings of Marx are all functions of the creation and sustenance of spaces of "reason-ability." The point is simply—and it is indeed a simple though fundamental point—that these words, and the effort required to write them, read them, and understand them, depend on the forces that produce them. They cannot sustain themselves. One might put it this way: self-consciousness is not self-sustaining.

Now, the most important point I wish to draw attention to here is that Marx, better than either Kant or Hegel, understands how his own efforts are contributions, not only to the *understanding* of the dynamics and telos of history, but to those dynamics and that telos themselves. This is evident in the kind of writing Marx engaged in—and my focus remains on the writings and not on the particular engagements that define his own life, his time on the planet, because it is his writings that engage us today. It is particularly evident in the text we are most concerned with, namely the *Communist Manifesto*, co-written with Friedrich Engels. It is, after all, a "manifesto," and not merely an exposition of ideas or even a proposal of ideas. It is an *affirmation* of its ideas, as ideas that need to be heard, and an *exhortation* to others to hear them. What else, after all, are we doing when we write, other than affirming something and exhorting others, however forcefully, to hear them? Are not "proposals" and "expositions" themselves, at bottom, just timid manifestos?

What are Marx's key affirmations? Given the concerns of this book, which lacks much of Marx's forcefulness but remains a manifesto nevertheless, we should start with: "The history of all hitherto existing society is the history of class struggles" (*Selected Writings*, p. 158). What I would like to point to in this affirmation is the use of the notion of "struggles." This notion contrasts with the notion of "conflict" that was the explicit concern of Kant, and was Hegel's concern as well. (In terms of speculative philosophy of history Hegel truly finds himself between Kant and Marx, some features of his thought tending towards a Kantian commitment to rationality and universality, while other features tend toward the Marxian commitment to the dynamics of a changing world.) The basic difference between the notion of "conflict" and that of "struggle" is that the former commits to something other than itself, namely, "resolution," whereas the latter remains committed only to itself, in the sense that it remains ongoing and does not resolve itself into something else. It seems to me that Marx, by focusing on "struggles," is closer to the *actual* movement of history, precisely because that movement does not resolve itself in something other than itself. History *is* an ongoing struggle.

But wait a minute: does not Marx's conception of history actually resolve itself into the classless society that he calls "communism" through the revolutionary work of the proletariat, which includes a form of dictatorship? This is all true, at least as far as Marx's "conception" of history abstractly considered is concerned. Such abstract concerns are not mine, however. My concern is with Marx's speculative philosophy of history, by which I mean the particular way in which his work helps us make better sense of the way in which the dynamics of history are articulated to its telos, such that we can better respond to the question of where we are headed. Such speculative work is called for precisely because we do not, indeed cannot, claim to *know*. Marx does not "know," any more than anyone else does, that history will resolve itself into a classless society. However, he does *anticipate* such a classless society and his writing is devoted to showing how, given his contact with the reality of *his* present and its particular orientation, and given the knowledge gained from examination of its past organization, his anticipations are well-founded.

Fine, I hear someone (many people) say, but history has proved Marx wrong, by which they mean that his anticipations have turned out not to have been well-founded. Not only have we not moved closer to a classless society, the very idea of creating a classless society has been thoroughly discredited. No one any longer anticipates such a society.

I am certainly prepared to grant that the anticipation of a classless society is not as predominant as it once was. However, what remains interesting about Marx's response is how forcefully it expresses the anticipatory dimension of speculative philosophy of history, the role that the future plays in the past-present-future complex. His philosophy tried to respond to the question at the heart of this book: where are we headed? If this is taken into consideration, we might then ask: if not towards a classless society, where are we headed? What can we anticipate, given the way we orient ourselves within our present as organized by its past? It seems to me that Marx remains relevant precisely *because* he focuses on how we orient ourselves within a world organized in particular ways and addresses the question of what we can anticipate or expect *given this particularity*. As we have seen, Hegel would also have us focus on the particularity of our present, but with more of a focus on its relation to the *universal*, rather than the *future*. What Marx brings to Hegel's account is an appeal to universality that provides a more sustained attention to the *anticipatory* dimension that consideration of the whole of history as the past-present-*future* complex demands.

In order to illustrate this, let me return to Marx's affirmation, but this time I will bracket the reference to "class," out of deference to the objection that no one now anticipates the "classless" society that this reference to class is arguably preparing us for. We get the following: "The history of all hitherto existing society is the history of [] struggles." This affirmation sounds somewhat odd. Now that we have taken the notion of "class" away, we are not quite sure what to make of the qualifier "hitherto existing," given that its function was to point to the particularity identified by the notion of class, which suggests that, if we are going to bracket the notion of "class," then we should bracket "hitherto existing" as well. Now what we get is: "The history of all [] society is the history of [] struggles."

Apart from my guess that many people would be perfectly happy with this pared-down affirmation, two things need to be noted. The first is that this pared-down affirmation is no less speculative than Marx's version. That is, we certainly do not *know* that this is the case, not, that is, if we think of history in terms of the past-present-future complex. The second point is that this pared-down affirmation is in itself not very interesting or informative. One immediately wants to ask: why? Why is the history of all society the history of struggles? Note that, if we take this question seriously, we will need to focus on the remaining terms, that is, either "society" or "history." The pared-down version, it seems to me, suggests that we look to the nature of "societies" in order to understand the constancy of the struggles within them. What if one focuses, not on the presumed "nature" of societies, but on their histories, recalling our discussion concerning the distinction between the social and the historical? That, of course, is precisely what Marx was doing, leading him to fill in the brackets.

The point of my little exercise here is to show that, even though Marx is usually discussed in terms of his understanding of the workings of class, as far as his speculative philosophy of history is concerned the interesting notion is that of "struggle." It is through the use of this notion that one can discern his attempt both to seize and to join the movement of history by situating himself within its present as structured by its past and pointing to its future.

Back to the *Manifesto*, then, and this initial basic affirmation that the dynamics of all "hitherto existing societies" have taken the shape of class struggles. I mentioned above that Marx, in using the notion of "struggle," better captures the actual movement of history, its dynamics, than does the use of the notion of "conflict." It does so because it is closer to that movement, as it were, which in fact is the movement of human life itself. Struggling is what being alive is all about. We struggle for air once we emerge from the struggling bodies of our mothers. We struggle to find places for ourselves within our families and in the wider social world. We struggle for what we desire, we struggle with our limitations and the limitations of others, we struggle for peace and justice, for peace and quiet, for happiness and fulfilment, for our lives.

However, to consider life as struggle, or even history as struggle, is too abstract. What shapes do those struggles take? Which ones are protracted? Which ones yield benefits? Think of speech. It is a struggle to speak, at first to speak at all, later to speak well, or before a group of people, or to a person whom one either loves or despises. It is not because we succeed in learning to speak that speaking ceases to be a struggle.

It is in this sense that the notion of "struggle" may be distinguished from the notion of "conflict." The latter, one might say, is a more specialized form of struggle, one that increasingly takes the form of an opposition between fairly well-defined positions, such as, for example, the Israeli–Palestinian conflict. When faced with a conflict, there are identifiable "sides," and one is called upon either to take sides, to mediate between them, or to stay out of the conflict altogether. This contrasts with the notion of a struggle, which one is called upon to join, or which one can abandon. When the two notions are contrasted in this way, one can see how the notion of struggle lends itself to the notion of movement in a way that the notion of conflict does not. In fact, the notion of conflict lends itself to a kind of stasis or paralysis rather than movement or, in its self-understanding, pretends to point beyond itself to a resolution that appeals, not to what inheres in the conflict itself, but to that which effectively transcends it. We might say that conflicts are struggles that have hardened into oppositions.

Now, Marx affirms that it is within "all *hitherto* existing societies" that class struggles describe the movement of history, which he also characterizes by saying (*Selected Writings*, p. 168): "All previous historical movements were movements of minorities, in the interests of minorities." Today, however, meaning in 1848, Marx and Engels affirm that the historical movements that have generated and sustained these class struggles have issued into a basic antagonism, indeed, a basic *confrontation* between two sides, which they famously describe as follows(*Selected Writings*, p. 159):

> In the earlier epochs of history, we find almost everywhere a complicated arrangement of society into various orders, a manifold gradation of social rank. In ancient Rome we have patricians, knights, plebeians, slaves; in the Middle Ages, feudal lords, vassals, guild-masters, journeymen, apprentices, serfs; in almost all of these classes, again, subordinate gradations.

> The modern bourgeois society that has sprouted from the ruins of feudal society has not done away with class antagonisms. It has but established new classes, new conditions of oppression, new forms of struggle in place of the old ones.

> Our epoch, the epoch of the bourgeoisie, possesses, however, this distinctive feature: it has simplified the class antagonisms. Society as a whole is more and more splitting up into two great hostile camps, into two great classes directly facing each other: Bourgeoisie and Proletariat.

What interests me in these passages is their speculative thrust and direction, that is, the way they combine the dynamics of history with its emerging telos. This is a process that we also saw in Hegel and that is required if we are to take history—as historical *movement*—seriously. Yet the first two paragraphs in the passage quoted above describe what amounts to a standard but nevertheless static conception of history, which merely catalogues the kinds of conflicts generated by different types of unequal social orders. I describe this as a static conception of history, not because nothing is happening—on the contrary, the conflicts generated can be quite spectacular—but because the agitation involved does not issue into a movement away from the inequality of the situation toward something that would eliminate, or at least correct, that inequality. Such agitation can issue into a radically altered social structure, but only to recreate another situation of conflict within a new social order, the re-establishing of, as Marx and Engels themselves put it, "new classes, new conditions of oppression, new forms of struggle in place of the old ones."

Such an anti-teleological conception of history is probably the norm today. It finds powerful expression in an often-quoted passage from Michel Foucault's essay "Nietzsche, Genealogy, History", which makes this Nietzschean affirmation (p. 378):

> Humanity does not gradually progress from combat to combat until it arrives at
> universal reciprocity, where the rule of law finally replaces warfare; humanity installs

each of its violences in a system of rules and thus proceeds from domination to domination.

However, I will point out, once again, the speculative character of such an affirmation—which, I might add, both Foucault and Nietzsche would have acknowledged. It may look like a statement of a more "realistic" approach to history, and it is, inasmuch as its focus is on the past. Yet, as a speculative affirmation, it speaks not only of the past but for the past-present-future complex as a whole. Foucault maintains that such forms of domination structure the past, are revealed in the present, *and* describe what we can expect from the future. Here it seems to me that the only honest response is to say, at least initially: maybe, maybe not. We certainly do not know.

Further, if we want to delve into these speculative matters a little more systematically, we can say, yes, as far as the past is concerned, it does show how different violences have been installed in systems of rules that have structured different forms of domination. However, if it makes sense to describe these different forms or structures of rule as different forms or structures of domination, then it makes sense to ask *what* is constantly being dominated in these changing systems. There is no reason to think that what is being dominated is always the same thing. The point is simply that, if we are to speculate about the constancy of domination, we are also committed to speculating about the constancy of being dominated. For the details of what is being dominated, one might follow Marx's suggestion and look at the shape of the struggles that have animated the lives of human beings within past societies. Countless historians across the planet are hard at work at precisely this task. However, given that we ourselves are concerned, not merely with the past, but with the past-present-future complex considered as a whole, we can also look at the struggles that animate the present, in order to see what future can be anticipated, given the particular characteristics of those present struggles.

It is against the backdrop of these kinds of concerns that we need to read the final paragraph in the quotation given above, Marx's (and Engels's) affirmation that "Society *as a whole* is more and more splitting up into two great hostile camps." Marx and Engels are writing a "manifesto" and thereby engaging themselves to do battle with one of the camps in question. That is, they are joining what they see as the basic or most general struggle going on in their present. Few today accept this basic dichotomous division of social life, in the name of pluralistic conditions of complexity (although, as we shall see in the next chapter, Michael Hardt and Antonio Negri seek to revitalize this Marxian way of characterizing the dynamics of social life without rejecting our pluralistic, complex, multicultural present). Nevertheless, the speculative dimension of this claim merits renewed consideration.

Marx and Engels are pointing to a movement within social life: society is *more and more* splitting into two. This is the vantage-point of the *present*. Within the struggles that human beings are "presently" engaged in one can see, not only the various conflicts that have been generated in the past when different interests confront each other, but an *orientation* that increasingly defines itself as overcoming a basic opposition. What makes this opposition basic is that, instead of the confrontation between different minority interests, which had been the source of countless conflicts in the past, what Marx and Engels were witnessing in their day was a radically new situation, one of opposition, not among various minority interests, but between minority interests themselves and the majority interest of all those who struggle to make a living. As I quoted earlier: "All previous historical movements were movements of minorities, or in the interest of minorities. The proletarian movement is the self-conscious, independent movement of the immense majority, in the interests of the immense majority." This is what the capitalist mode of organizing social life is achieving in its pursuit of ever greater riches and wealth: the creation of a class of the immense majority, whose interests lie, not in the exploitation of another class, but in the elimination of class interests *per se*. Thus, for Marx and Engels, the dynamics of the productive forces as organized under capitalist exploitation take on a very distinctive shape and direction (*Selected Writings*, p. 176):

> When, in the course of development, class distinctions have disappeared and all production has been concentrated in the hands of a vast association of the whole nation, the public power will lose its political character. Political power, properly so called, is merely the organized power of one class for oppressing another. If the proletariat during its contest with the bourgeoisie is compelled, by force of circumstances, to organize itself as a class, and, as such, sweeps away by force the old conditions of production, then it will, along with these conditions, have swept away the conditions for the existence of class antagonisms and of classes generally, and will thereby have abolished its own supremacy as a class.

Thus, close attention to the actual dynamics of historical movement—the pitting of bourgeois class interests in increasing profits and wealth against the emerging class(less) interests of a self-associating productive proletariat—reveals the telos of history itself:

> In the place of the old bourgeois society, with its classes and class antagonisms, we shall have an association, in which the free development of each is the condition for the free development of all.

This intimate link between the dynamics of history and its telos is also neatly captured in another famous passage from Marx, from his *Critique of the Gotha Programme* (*Selected Writings*, p. 321):

> In a higher phase of communist society, after the enslaving subordination of the individual to the division of labour has vanished; after labour has become not only a means of life but life's prime want; after the productive forces have also increased with the all-round development of the individual, and all of the springs of common wealth flow more abundantly—only then can the narrow horizon of bourgeois right be crossed in its entirety and society inscribe on its banners: "From each according to his abilities, to each according to his needs!"

While this is often taken to be a "utopian" passage, describing a hoped-for but unlikely future, it should be read more simply as an anticipatory description of the processes at work in the present, given our capitalistically organized past. It anticipates the end of enslavement and an imposed division of labour, a conception of work linked to one's desires, a commitment to an "all-round" development of individuals, and the sharing of the wealth collectively produced. (We shall see in the next chapter how those anticipations continue to be ours, that is, how they continue to structure the past-present-future complex as it is lived.)

Of course, someone is sure to point out here that neither the passage from the *Manifesto* nor the one from the *Critique* captures what happened. The dynamics of history did not polarize society into two antagonistic classes, issuing into a revolutionary movement that transformed society into a classless society. There have been revolutions, of course, but they did not pit minority interests against a supposed interest of the "immense majority" in the way Marx hoped and envisioned.

Marx and Engels provide the appropriate response to this observation in the very *Manifesto* we are here considering as a piece of speculative philosophy of history (*Selected Writings*, p. 171): "In bourgeois society . . . the past dominates the present; in communist society, the present dominates the past." Indeed, the objections raised to Marxian speculative philosophy of history and to speculative philosophy of history generally, are often objections that appeal to what has happened in the past. While it is crucial not to ignore what has happened in the past, we need to remind ourselves that the past forms only one component in the past-present-future complex. We need also to consider our present contact with reality and our anticipations with regard to the future. We need to ask whether or not, in our objections, we are projecting our pasts onto the future. When we do so we are in fact failing our present. Or, to put it in terms of the modal square within which our lives unfold, we should not confuse the necessities exhibited by the past with the possibilities (and impossibilities) that structure our relation to the future.

It is true that we cannot say a great deal about the future, because we do not *know* what it holds, but we do not say nothing at all. We include statements about the future in our anticipatory understanding of the movements that carry us out of the past, through the present, and into the future. Marx had a fairly good appreciation of this overall dynamic. Indeed, as he and Engels put it in another co-written text, *The German Ideology*, the notion of "communism" is meant to capture, both in theory and in practice—that is, in a social-practical sense—the anticipatory dimension of the unfolding of our social lives. They write (*Selected Writings*, p. 120):

> Communism is not for us a *state of affairs* still to be established, not an *ideal* to which reality [will] have to adjust. We call communism the *real* movement which abolishes the present state of affairs.

This reference to "the real movement" is what we should focus on. Communism as real movement challenges our tendency to view the present, or the present state of affairs, in abstraction from the past-present-future complex, as though it were self-contained and self-explanatory strictly on its own terms, the familiar terms it uses in order to understand itself.

Consider, for example, the distribution of wealth all around one. On a street corner, at a stop-light, one may find cars whose cost rivals the prices of small houses, public transit buses, taxis, bicycles, and people on foot, including some pushing grocery carts filled with their "worldly" belongings. One might think that these things, these people, merely bear witness in a particular way to a world that perennially divides the rich and the poor, and that contact with them in the "present" captures something essential and permanent about human existence. While the desire to find in one's existence evidence of what is essential and permanent about human existence itself is perfectly understandable, and the source of much philosophical speculation, one needs only a minimal sense of history, of things changing because of the different ways in which people have responded to the conditions that confronted them, to suggest that what has been deemed permanent and essential is in fact the product of the particular way in which historical circumstances have been dealt with.

If we go back to our street corner and wonder, not about the variations in the wealth of the individuals one encounters there, but about what they are all doing and where they are going, then the specifically historical circumstances that engage them cannot be ignored. We are at a stop-light that regulates the flow of traffic, produced by the concentration of people within a city or town, formed or coalesced around various economic activities, productive of particular goods and services that are distributed in highly specific ways. Although the people sitting in the cars and buses, standing, walking, or huddled in a doorway may physically resemble human beings across the world and through time, the way in which they relate to each other in what they are doing has the specificity of history, rather than the (presumed) permanence of nature. As Marx puts it, in the first volume of *Capital* (*Selected Writings*, p. 266):

> nature does not produce on the one hand owners of money or commodities, and on the other hand men possessing nothing other than their own labour-power. This relation has no basis in natural history, nor does it have a social basis common to all periods of human history. It is clearly the result of a past historical development, the product of many economic revolutions, of the extinction of a whole series of older formations of social production.

Thus, on Marx's account, communism should not be understood as a future abstracted from the present, but as an anticipatory understanding of the most significant developmental movement *within* the present, as that present has been structured by the discernable movements of the past. For Marx, the most significant developmental movement is a mode of organization that has created not only the conditions of its own suppression as rule based on private property, but also the possibility of a form of association of the productive forces of society that will not rely on a form of rule alien to those productive forces. In the *Manifesto* Marx and Engels describe the developmental situation in the following way (*Selected Writings*, p. 169):

> The essential condition for the existence, and for the sway of the bourgeois class, is the formation and augmentation of capital; the condition for capital is wage-labour. Wage-labour rests exclusively on competition between the labourers. The advance of industry, whose involuntary promoter is the bourgeoisie, replaces the isolation of the labourers, due to competition, by their revolutionary combination, due to association. The development of Modern Industry, therefore, cuts from under its feet the very foundation on which the bourgeoisie produces and appropriates products. What the bourgeoisie, therefore, produces, above all, is its own grave-diggers. Its fall and the victory of the proletariat are equally inevitable.

We need to recall that this passage is taken from a "manifesto," one which ends famously with the cry: "WORKING MEN OF ALL COUNTRIES, UNITE!" It is in such a context that we need to make sense of the claim that the fall of bourgeois rule and the victory of the proletariat are equally "inevitable."

One cannot dismiss such a phrase as mere rhetorical flourish, especially if we consider other famous passages in Marx's writings, such as in his *Preface to a Contribution to the Critique of Political Economy* (*Selected Writings*, p. 211):

> At a certain stage of development, the material productive forces of society come into conflict with the existing relations of production or—this merely expresses the same thing in legal terms—with the property relations within the framework of which they have operated hitherto. From forms of development of the productive forces these relations turn into their fetters. Then begins an era of social revolution. The changes in the economic foundation lead sooner or later to the transformation of the whole immense superstructure. . . . No social formation is ever destroyed before all the productive forces for which it is sufficient have been developed, and new superior relations of production never replace older ones before the material conditions for their existence have matured within the framework of the old society. Mankind thus *inevitably* [my emphasis] sets itself only such tasks as it is able to solve, since closer examination will always show that the problem itself arises only when the material conditions for its solution are already present, or at least in the course of formation.

It has often been noted that there seems to be a tension in Marx's thought, between such assertions about the "inevitability" of a transformation of social relations, so that the productive forces they embody are organized in a way that benefits all producers and not merely those who control the means of production, and his critical, practical engagement in arguing for the proletariat's historical role in that transformation. If the transformation is "inevitable," and involves the unification of the workers as a function of the real, material process of historical development, why the exhortation to workers to "unite"? In other words, is there not a determinism in Marx's thought, which by now has been thoroughly discredited?

Rather than worry about determinism, I think it would be more worthwhile to examine more closely what it might mean to consider what is "inevitable" within the historical process understood as the past-present-future complex. Technically, of course, something is "inevitable" when one cannot avoid it. It is difficult to make claims about what is "inevitable" when one is thinking about the future, given the present and its particular past, but it is not impossible, or, at least, not unintelligible.

For example, it is inevitable that each of us will one day die. Death is not something we can avoid. That does not mean that we need to welcome it or embrace or hasten it. Indeed, we may even take steps to avoid it, for the time being, even though we know that we will not avoid it in the long run. Note also that we do not know how we will die (leaving questions as they pertain to taking one's own life aside), even though we know that it is inevitable.

If we keep this in mind, then the suggestion is that the victory of the proletariat and the reorganization of productive forces around an associational model is "inevitable" in the sense that, given the way our present has been structured by its past, it cannot be avoided. Now, one can well imagine that, as with death, all kinds of steps will be taken to avoid it for the time being, most notably by the bourgeoisie, whose fall is being announced. One can even imagine how members of the proletariat may avoid victory by failing to recognize themselves as part of the solution to a problem that they do not cast in appropriately historical terms. One can imagine any number of "avoidance strategies" that defer our encounter with the "inevitable," in much the same way that, even as adults, we avoid responsibilities, engagements or promises that we should otherwise recognize, or, indeed, often do recognize, but incompletely, or opaquely, or uncourageously. The "inevitable" in our developing human lives is unknowable because it lies in the future, and yet it demands a response from us.

What is interesting and important about Marx's response is that it is meant to include us all, understood as all of us who struggle for the conditions of the realization of all, and this in contrast to those who focus on the interests of only some of us. That is, Marx's response concerns an historically specific, historically defined universality, based on the actual productive forces that actually drive social life forward, and not an abstract universality that somehow transcends the actual struggle of historical movement. It is not even the universality of those whom Marx and Engels called the "critical-utopian socialists," who (*Selected Writings*, p. 183) "consider themselves far superior to all class antagonisms" and "want to improve the condition of every member of society, even that of the most favoured." It is the universality that emerges from that historical struggle that Marx deems "inevitable" and that can no longer be avoided if one takes history seriously. Indeed, recognition of this inevitability is largely avoided precisely by efforts *not* to take history seriously enough.

At the heart of Marx's attempt to make sense of his world was his commitment to taking history, understood as the past-present-future complex considered as a whole, seriously. To take history seriously is, in my view, to recognize, as Marx did, that, as he put it in another famous passage, this from *The Eighteenth Brumaire of Louis Bonaparte* (*Selected Writings*, p. 188):

> Men make their own history, but they do not make it just as they please; they do not make it under circumstances chosen by themselves, but under circumstances directly encountered, given and transmitted from the past.

Those "circumstances directly encountered" describe the present-in-contact as this has been shaped by the past and as it is directed to the future in the anticipations that such a present allows us to envisage. To call such anticipations "inevitable" is to point resolutely to that future, as it outlines itself in the labouring and productive forces of human lives, struggling with the fetters imposed on them by those who would control them through the regulation of their activities, through the imposition of a form on those activities that does not issue forth from the activities themselves, as history itself does. Thus the human activities that are literally the very subject of history—the motor, the dynamics of historical movement—point beyond their particular given forms to a mode of *inter*-activity that Marx identifies as *self-activity* (*Selected Writings*, p. 152): "The transformation of labour into self-activity corresponds to the transformation of the previous restricted interaction into the interaction of individuals as such." It is this transformation that Marx deems to be "inevitable," that is, unavoidable.

The speculative force of Marx's reading of history considered as a whole remains powerful, as I will attempt to show in the next chapter. Before doing that, however, I want to address one last consideration on the "inevitability" of the telos of history as identified by Marx. If Marx meant to describe the "inevitable" realization of the free development of each and therefore of all as in some sense a *necessary* process, then he was modally confused. As we saw in the Introduction to this book, necessity is not a modal category that applies to the future, considered as a component of the past-present-future complex. What we confront when we confront the future are not necessities, but *possibilities*, against the backdrop of impossibilities. Of course, we need to deal with the necessities of the past, which we cannot change, but we do so in a contingent present, in the sense that *things could have been otherwise* if human beings had taken different courses of action, within circumstances that could have presented themselves otherwise than they in fact did. Of course, human beings did take the actions they did within the circumstances as they did present themselves, and therefore, from the perspective of a contingent present, things in the past are *of necessity* the way that they are. However, the past issues into a present that itself *could be otherwise* and therefore presents itself as *contingently* what it is.

It is with these considerations in mind that one must read Marx's famous Eleventh Thesis, in his *Theses on Feuerbach* (*Selected Writings*, p. 101): "The philosophers have only *interpreted* the world in various ways; the point is to *change* it." If philosophers have restricted themselves to interpreting the world, it is because they have focused their attention on the world as it *was*, abstracted from their present engagement, and construed as an object independent of the philosophers themselves and their contemplative stances. However, the world as it *is*, as it presents itself to our engaged activity, is not independent of our efforts to make our way within it. It is an historical world structured as a past-present-future complex, to which we bear a contingent relationship.

Now, interestingly, this contingent relation to the world as it unfolds is one that we all share, and in that sense it is "inevitable." Indeed, one might go further and insist that proper attention to the historical context within which we live out our lives points to the "inevitably" contingent demands and features of this shared world. It is this odd conjunction of the "inevitable" and the "contingent" that best illustrates what it means to live in an historical world, that is, a world that has taken on a particular shape that, though it could have been otherwise, is in fact what it is, and that, *because* it is what it is, and not what it could otherwise have been, raises the question of what it might become in the continuing course of time. This question is not an abstract one, though of course it is a speculative one. It is a question about how this present world will develop and unfold, given our contingent relation to it. It is the anticipatory question that forms part of a full appreciation of the past-present-*future* complex that is history considered as a whole.

This emphasis on the contingent is fundamental to much contemporary postmodern political theorizing which, though appreciative of Marx's commitment to not merely interpret the world but to change it, generally rejects his overall speculative framework. I think that this is a mistake or, rather, I think that it is a mistake to read the effort to provide a speculative philosophy of history, in order to help us make sense of where we are headed, as insisting on the unfolding *necessity* of the historical process. The point of speculative philosophy of history is to help us articulate our anticipations of the actual structures and movements of history, as we encounter them contingently in the present. The postmodern insistence and emphasis on presenting the social and political configurations of the world as contingently constituted is, then, appropriate, given the modal context of an historical world. It is a mistake to think that the way things are in the present is the way they have to be.

William E. Connolly, for example, seems to me to be quite right to insist on seeing, in any given present conjunction or "conglomeration" of events, the many contingent elements that are at play. This is how he describes the different contingent elements that circumscribe the situation of what are called "illegal aliens" in the Southwestern United States, bordering on Mexico, in a passage in his book *Neuropolitics* (pp. 151–152):

> . . . the geographic border between Mexico and the United States created by past wars, the asymmetrical development of the two economies, the structure of the fast-food and agricultural economy in the American Southwest, the organization of illegal entry strategies, the entanglement of the border in the drug trade and an American war on drugs inside and outside the country, the tax and welfare system of the United States, and the racialization and territorialization of ethnic divisions within and around the working class . . .

Following a certain reading of Foucault, Connolly refuses to see in this conjunction of factors an overarching or underlying intelligibility. He wants us instead to focus on what "emerges" from this conjunction, which he identifies as "a powerful contrivance of economic discipline and political separation." His point, again following a certain reading of Foucault, is the following:

> No central power intended it, even though it is bound together by the diverse
> intentions of agents at multiple sites with differential power. And yet, once it emerges
> as a contingent constellation, a variety of constituencies caught in it face powerful
> pressures to adjust their goals, strategies, and interests to its limits and possibilities.

The point of insisting on the constellation as *contingent*, even as it is constraining, is to enable us to conceive of these constraints as fluid, allowing for the possibility of free movement within them and, of course, against them (this is also something stressed by Foucault). Connolly opposes the contingent to the necessary. He calls such a constellated situation a "contraption," which he defines as "a loosely structured *modus vivendi* crafted out of complex relays," built out of disparate intentionalities that are affect-laden and which, as relays, connect the "conglomeration" or "contrivance" through (and note how he tracks the description above):

> . . . the pain of refugees, armed border patrols, the market power of corporate
> elites, the ideological stratification of market forces, the demands of consumers,
> the difficulties traditional blue-collar workers have in making ends meet, the
> mobilization of layered identity anxieties, the identification of drugs crossing the
> border with the decline of public morality, widespread frustration with a tax system
> that does not serve the needs of ordinary people and interventions by the state . . .

Connolly insistently refuses to see in this "contraption," this political "contrivance," a whole understood as a totality working itself out, principally because, like Foucault, he wishes to situate himself *within* the struggles that constitute key features of elements of this "contraption." Generally, I would agree. It would certainly be a mistake to pass over the various elements that Connolly so ably identifies in his reconstruction of this "contraption." It is also important to see in them, not a necessary process, but the contingent result of events and actions that certainly could have gone on otherwise.

Having said that, if we are attempting to understand a situation, or "contraption," like that of "illegal aliens" in the Southwestern United States, then we cannot merely rest content with noting its contingent features. Connolly refuses to see any underlying intelligible process working itself out, but, as his careful description shows, he does not eschew intelligibility *per se*.

His descriptions still attempt to *make sense* of the situation. Indeed, to call the situation a "contraption" is precisely to give it a certain sense or meaning, which allows us to ask: how exactly does this contraption work?

Connolly's strategy is to track the "relays" he identifies, in the hope of producing a clearer picture of the salient features of the situation that may enable us to better understand and deal with it. Yet this is exactly what speculative philosophy of history means to contribute to. What it seeks to do is put the "contraptions" that Connolly identifies into a wider historical context, speculatively reconstructed as a past-present-future complex. If one looks at his characterization of the "relays" connecting the disparate elements, one can discern without too much ideological spin a fairly basic and straightforward *struggle* over the way in which vested interests control "the terms of political discourse" (itself the title of an earlier book by Connolly) in order to make use of those "forces of production and reproduction" without which those interests would no longer be "vested." (The Marxian phrase "forces of production and reproduction" seems to me to be perfectly appropriate here and, as we shall see, elsewhere too.) To put it another way, the complex layerings and relays that Connolly helpfully and importantly traces and tracks should not replace attention to what can also be helpfully and importantly identified as an underlying basic struggle. We should at least be able to see such basic features, without being charged with reductionism and/or ideological posturing. That basic struggle is the struggle to live through the concrete possibilities that current modes of living together promote and prevent and prepare. After all, Connolly's topic here is "illegal aliens," a term that refers to *labouring* human beings. Reference to that activity in characterizing the functioning of the constellated situation is, surely, *the* focus around which the other contingent elements coalesce. It seems to me important to be able to identify focal and peripheral points in discussions of this kind, in order to evaluate and weigh different responses to and within the "contraption" under examination.

In other words, there seems to be a kind of ahistoricism in Connolly's account, which does not sit well with his otherwise valiant and, I believe, penetrating attempt to be timely. It seems to me that the desire to be timely would be best served by speculative considerations of historical time, in terms of both the dynamics of its unfolding and the telos that it identifies. Indeed, one might argue that Connolly's characterization of the "contraption" within which "illegal aliens" are caught itself presumes the telos that Marx identifies as the free development of each and therefore of all. If the focus of Connolly's concern, within the complex relays that he identifies, is the plight of the illegal aliens, in the sense that it is they who face the most powerful pressures to "adjust their goals, strategies, and interests," it is because it is the illegal aliens themselves who, through their struggle, most powerfully resist those pressures.

They resist in the name, not of their particular interests, but of what Étienne Balibar, in his "Ambiguous Universality" (p. 64), calls the "ideal universality" of the insurgent, by which he means "those who collectively rebel against domination in the name of freedom and equality." Such an "ideal" universality contrasts with the "real" universality discussed in Part I in connection with Kant and with the way in which history has overtaken the cosmopolitan ideal by rendering its "regulative status" questionable. However, it also contrasts with the form of universality discussed in connection with the spaces of "reasonability" that Hegel's account of mutual recognition sought to emphasize.

What Balibar means by "ideal" universality is a universality that has emerged out of the historical movement that emphasizes and affirms, continuously and repeatedly, the "equality" and "freedom" of all human beings to live out their lives as best they can. Balibar insists on the fact that *both* "equality" and "freedom" are proclaimed for all, that both notions stand or fall together, in what he terms the "equaliberty" of human beings. This is the telos issuing from the dynamics of historical movement. It echoes Marx's telos of free development, inasmuch as, according to Balibar (p. 66), it needs to be considered as "trans-individual," in the following sense:

> Rights of equality and liberties are indeed *individual*: only individuals can claim and support them. But the combined suppression of coercion and discrimination (which we may call emancipation) is always clearly a *collective process*, which can be achieved only if many individuals (virtually all of them) unite and join efforts against oppression and social hierarchies.

Balibar's telos can be further likened to Marx's in its "inevitability." That is, even though Balibar calls the form of universality that it describes "ideal," he makes it clear (pp. 66–67) that this

> is not to say that it does not play an active role (or that there are no processes of emancipation). What we observe is rather is that the ideal of non-discrimination and non-coercion is "immortal" or irrepressible, that it is revived again and again in different situations, but also that it is continuously displaced in history.

I think it is possible to understand this "irrepressible" demand for "equaliberty" as being akin to Marx's sense of the "inevitable" victory of the proletariat as the standard-bearers of such "equaliberty." As we shall see in the next chapter, a similar case is put forward in the work of Michael Hardt and Antonio Negri.

6

The Biopolitical Production of the Common

The previous chapter was devoted to trying to show how Marx's speculative response to our question of where we are headed remains relevant. The telos of the free development of all can indeed be seen to be an ultimate direction or end that manifests itself at the heart of the basic struggle that animates the dynamics of social life. It is the demonstrated intimacy of the telos and the dynamics within Marx's understanding of, and engagement with, history that is, in my view, most significant. Marx shows how history reveals to us an unfolding world in which our individual commitments to making a life for ourselves, and the struggles that ensue, pit our common struggle to do so against structural forms of organization that prevent the free development of those forces, our own productive efforts, in order to appropriate them in the interests of a few. These are the dynamics of history. Because these dynamics engage all of us, Marx allows us at the same time to see, through that engagement, the end (the telos) of that engagement: the free development of our own productive forces in the interests of all. For Marx the dynamics and the telos of history are one and the same, the former viewed from within the context of our present, the latter viewed according to our anticipations, given that present as illuminated by our understanding of the past.

I doubt that many people will be persuaded by my claim that this reading of Marx does indeed tell us where we are headed. However, persuasion is not my goal. This is a philosophical investigation and is less concerned with persuading others of a truth that it possesses than with insisting on exploring a question that merits our consideration. If the reader has stayed with me this far I assume that it is because the consideration I have been giving to the question is not without some resonance in his or her thinking. Rather than give a "persuasive" response to the question I have posed, my aim is to give more shape and substance to the "nagging feeling" I identified in the Introduction, which I translated into the form of our question: where are we headed?

However, I do not want to appear to be trying to make things easier for myself. If I mention the possibility of a lack of persuasion, it is because I do not think that Marx's response to our question is sufficient. The test, of course, is the test that I have urged the reader to take whenever he or she deems it appropriate: to look up from the texts we are discussing and look at the world as it presents itself, to see if it makes any more sense, given consideration of those texts. That is not the same as putting the books aside and returning to what one was doing before opening them. We sometimes need to do that too, but it is not a test of them.

Obviously, for my part, I do think that the world makes more sense after having considered Marx's response to our question, but also after considering the responses of Kant and Hegel as well—so much so that I have engaged in the writing of this accompanying text. However, as I also noted in the Introduction, along with this "nagging feeling" that we are headed somewhere that needs to be thought about, the world as it presents itself today also has a distinguishing feature that we should consider in responding to this "nagging feeling." I identified this distinguishing feature as the fact that the world is becoming increasingly multicultural. To notice that the world is becoming increasingly multicultural is to notice that it is *changing* in a distinguishable way. The question about where we are headed is concerned with the direction of that change. Like Hegel and Kant before him, Marx has provided us a framework, not only for understanding our changing world, but for engaging it.

What I wish to do in this final chapter is show how Marx's framework, suitably updated, can help us better make sense of the fact that the world is becoming increasingly multicultural, in a way that allows us to deepen the insights about where we are headed. I shall do so by discussing two co-authored texts published recently by Michael Hardt and Antonio Negri, *Empire* and *Multitude*. (I should mention that much of this chapter takes up matters I discussed in my article "Moving Beyond Biopower," published in 2005.)

Some have called Hardt and Negri a latter-day Marx and Engels, and hailed their work as a new *Communist Manifesto*. I shall be treating them in this way myself because I believe that they do indeed provide us with a contemporary version of the kind of "manifesto" that Marx and Engels intended, a document that would describe a shared reality and serve as a rallying cry to participation in the movement of that reality. More importantly for my own little "manifesto" here, Hardt and Negri allow us to make better sense of our multicultural world in terms of its present dynamics and telos.

MULTICULTURAL DYNAMICS AND THE ENDS OF HISTORY

Like the *Communist Manifesto*, the works of Hardt and Negri are meant to provide an alternative description of reality. They seek to counter both the positive ideal of "perpetual peace" and the negative ideal of a "clash of civilizations," both of which shun the actual movement of history. Similarly, Marx and Engels in their own day wanted to counter what they called "nursery tales," specifically (Marx, *Selected Writings*, p. 158) the nursery tale of "the Spectre of Communism." How does one counter, or rather "meet," such a nursery tale?

There is nothing inherently wrong with nursery tales. They rock us to sleep, and allow our minds to twirl pleasantly about and occasionally be thrilled. Crucially, however, such tales are told to us, they are not things we tell each other. To counter them, to "meet" them, is to speak to one another, rather than have some tell stories to others. This is important for understanding history and our engagement with history. Do we want history to tell us stories, or do we want history to be a way of speaking to one another? Indeed, the same goes for scientific research generally. Do we want some of us to tell others how things are in the world, or do we want to discover the workings of the world alongside one another? Thus, both the *Communist Manifesto*, on the one hand, and *Empire* and *Multitude*, on the other, are attempts to speak, and not attempts to tell a story. Both use stories that are told in order to speak, stories that are told as history, as opposed to history told as stories.

For Marx and Engels, as we have seen, "The history of all hitherto existing society is the history of class struggles." Sociology has for a long time been constituted around understanding the social world in terms of classificatory schema, with some sociologists seeking to show how social orders function, while others have more "dialectical" intentions, hoping to see in the divisions of the world a movement working itself out. Much seems to hang on whether the emphasis is placed on "classes," with their particular barriers and determined sets of possibilities, or on the struggles that animate them. As we saw in the previous chapter, it is pretty clear from the *Communist Manifesto* that Marx and Engels's focus is on the basic struggle that, because it is so basic, allows us to define once and for all the movement that will enable us to go beyond the appropriation of the fruits of that struggle by the few (*Selected Writings*, p. 159):

> Our epoch, the epoch of the bourgeoisie, possesses, however, this distinctive feature:
> it has simplified the class antagonisms. Society is *more and more* [my emphasis]
> splitting up into two great hostile camps, into two great classes directly facing each
> other: Bourgeoisie and Proletariat.

Our epoch may not have exactly the same shape as the epoch described by Marx and Engels, but it seems to me that much of what Hardt and Negri are doing in their two books amounts to reminding us that we too are living in an "epoch," living *in* history, not as stories that some tell to others, but as a *time* with distinctive features, which we need to assume as our own. For Marx and Engels the distinctive feature was that "more and more," a becoming (clearer), an animating force that they were attempting to put into words. The same is true of Hardt and Negri. A focus on this "more and more" will reveal the great face-to-face encounter between "Empire" and "the multitude," for the two books that bear these terms as their titles are portraits, descriptions of these two faces that face each other, perhaps not yet looking each other in the eye, even when not seeing things eye to eye, still being evasive and uncertain. Hence the need to focus.

The confrontation between "Empire" and "multitude" is a reactualization of the confrontation between bourgeoisie and proletariat, but it is a reactualization in a different "epoch," one whose movements have taken on different shapes and different dynamics. The core notion of a basic struggle defined by a basic confrontation remains, but for Hardt and Negri this confrontation is no longer to be understood "dialectically," that is, as driven by contradiction, resolved through negation and reconstituting a "higher" unity or synthesis. What then is the remaining character of the basic confrontation?

For Marx the bourgeoisie represented a revolutionary movement within history that transformed society by appropriating the fruits of productive labour through its control and ownership of the means of production. The consolidation of that movement and the interests that it served was realized in a particular form of rule, typically articulated in the rule of law as institutionalized within and through the structures of what were understood as sovereign nation-states. What Hardt and Negri want to point out, especially in *Empire*, is that the deployment of the form of rule that accompanies and consolidates capitalist exploitation has taken on a form that explodes the consolidation of these earlier institutional forms. Capitalist exploitation of the productive forces of society continues, but the consolidation of that exploitation has taken on a different form, which they propose to name "Empire" given that it is an imperial rather than a "state" form of rule. Although it is an imperial form of rule, "Empire" is not imperial*ism* (*Empire*, pp. xii–xiii):

> Empire establishes no territorial center of power and does not rely on fixed
> boundaries or barriers. It is a *decentred* and *deterritorializing* apparatus of rule that
> progressively incorporates the entire global realm within its open, expanding frontiers
> . . . Empire manages hybrid identities, flexible hierarchies, and plural exchanges
> through modulating networks of command. The distinct national colours of the

imperialist map of the world have merged and blended in the imperial global rainbow.

This colourful style of writing is typical of both *Empire* and *Multitude*, as are the inserts within each text that cut up the narrative/argument by returning to certain themes by way of sometimes idiosyncratic allusions to various historical and literary figures. Such stylistic flourishes have apparently profoundly irritated Hardt and Negri's critics, and yet it seems to me that they are perfectly appropriate to their attempt to make sense of a world that is changing, in ways that are insufficiently recognized by standard modes of argument. Like Marx and Engels, Hardt and Negri are self-consciously involved and engaged in their writing, and not simply attempting to communicate some kind of timeless thought. Indeed, this attempt to grasp or rather to follow the movement of a changing world is precisely what Empire does as well, but in the mode of consolidating its power to rule and impose its order on this changing world.

This is a key feature of Empire: its strategy is to consolidate its rule by matching the movement of social productive forces while denying its own historicity. According to Hardt and Negri, from the point of view of the consolidation of a particular world order that preserves the hold that capitalist forms of exploitation have on the productive forces, a consolidation that they attempt to make sense of by means of what they call the "concept" of Empire, the shape of the world looks like this (*Empire*, pp. xiv–xv):

> The concept of Empire is characterized fundamentally by a lack of boundaries:
> Empire's rule has no limits. First and foremost, then, the concept of Empire posits
> a regime that effectively encompasses the spatial totality, or really that rules over the
> entire "civilized" world. No territorial boundaries limit its reign. Second, the concept
> of Empire presents itself not as a historical regime originating in conquest, but rather
> as an order that effectively suspends history and thereby fixes the existing state of
> affairs for eternity. From the perspective of Empire, this is the way things will always
> be and the way they were always meant to be. In other words, Empire presents its
> rule not as a transitory moment in the movement of history, but as a regime with
> no temporal boundaries and in this sense outside of history or at the end of history.
> Third, the rule of Empire operates on all registers of the social order extending
> down to the depths of the social world. Empire not only manages a territory and a
> population, but also creates the very world it inhabits. It not only regulates human
> interactions, but also seeks directly to rule over human nature. The object of its
> rule is social life in its entirety, and thus Empire presents the paradigmatic form of
> biopower. Finally, although the practice of Empire is continually bathed in blood,
> the concept of Empire is always dedicated to peace—a perpetual and universal peace
> outside of history.

There are a couple of things that need to be noted here if we want to continue reading Hardt and Negri as in some sense updating and, I would claim, correcting Marx's speculative philosophy of history, in which the movement of history generates its telos. First, though Hardt and Negri write of the "concept" of Empire, and are intent on "theorizing" our contemporary world by means of it, I think that it is a mistake to try to find a "theory" of Empire in their work. Rather than producing a "theory," they are concerned with "theorizing" what they believe can be discerned as (*Empire*, p. xi) an emerging "global order, a new logic and structure of rule—in short, a new form of sovereignty." Their theorizing efforts are concerned with making sense of a changing world in terms of the emergence of a "new logic and structure of rule," which they call Empire, but which at the same time allows them to articulate the forces that are ruled in terms of something they call "the multitude." Their object of concern is the dynamic interaction between the emergence of a particular form of rule and the forces that are ruled by it.

We would do well to conceive of Hardt and Negri's effort to "theorize" the changing conditions of our contemporary world as an example of what Michael Oakeshott calls, in his *On Human Conduct*, the exploration of the "conditional platform of understanding" that expresses itself in what people are doing in a given time and place. Oakeshott reminds us (p. 1) that:

> Understanding is not such that we either enjoy it or lack it altogether. To be human and to be aware is to encounter only what is in some manner understood. Thus, it may be said that understanding is an unsought condition; we inexorably inhabit a world of intelligibles. But understanding as an engagement is an exertion; it is the resolve to inhabit an ever more intelligible or an ever less mysterious world. This unconditional engagement of understanding I shall call "theorizing." It is an engagement to abate mystery rather than to achieve definitive understanding.

The point I wish to draw from Oakeshott is his concern with intelligibility. Theorizing has an unconditional commitment to intelligibility. That is, it interrogates a world, which, as a world, is always a world of particular intelligibles, but whose intelligibility is unsatisfying to the intelligence that engages it. A particular intelligence can of course be too quickly satisfied with the intelligibility of the world that it inhabits, but, insofar as it is, that intelligence is not engaged in "theorizing."

The world, then, for Hardt and Negri is most intelligible when it is understood as the "biopolitical" production of Empire/multitude. To use Oakeshott's vocabulary one more time, this is the "theorem," emerging from the enterprise of theorizing, that they propose. From their theorizing of the intelligible structures of "the world" emerges this theorem of Empire/multitude.

The particular characteristics of the theorizing effort of Hardt and Negri and the object of their world indicate that what they are involved in can best be described as speculative philosophy of history, because their primary concern is with the movement of our changing world as well as its direction. These are the traditional concerns of speculative philosophy of history. Given the particular characteristics of imperial rule, Hardt and Negri seem especially concerned with reactivating the sense of history that, they argue, is in fact occluded by the emerging world order. This reactivation of history as discernable and intelligible movement seems to be overlooked by many of their critics, such as Ian Angus, who argues (in his article "Empire, Borders, Place") that, for Hardt and Negri, there is no "outside" to Empire and thus no way of imagining a transcending of it. However, what Hardt and Negri are precisely trying to do by identifying the state of the world in terms of Empire is, as they explicitly assert (*Empire*, p. xvi), to provide "a general theoretical framework and a toolbox of concepts for theorizing and acting in and against Empire."

I would like to suggest that we can get a better sense of what is of value and importance in what they are doing by following Foucault and treating Empire—or rather Empire/multitude, which better expresses the dynamic that animates this "concept"—as a "principle of intelligibility" (as discussed in Foucault's *Sécurité, Territoire, Population*, pp. 294–295). What Foucault means when he invokes a "principle of intelligibility" is akin to Kant's use of the notion of a "regulative idea," that is, something that governs and structures the organization of thought. Of course, Foucault is not engaged in the same project as Kant is. His concern is not with establishing and articulating the conditions of objectivity *per se*, but rather with examining historically the ways in which things coalesce and make sense in the particular ways that they do—hence the appeal to the notion of intelligibility. The idea of a principle of intelligibility is meant to capture the movement of thought at a given time that gathers around and is structured around, or coalesces around, certain ways of making sense of privileged objects of concern. A principle of intelligibility describes the object, the goal, and the foundation of a particular exercise of reason or reasoning at a given time, arising out of specific conditions and responding to those conditions. One example Foucault develops is that of the state as this arose in the sixteenth and seventeenth centuries. The movements of thought around conceptualizing the state at this time were, according to Foucault, as significant for understanding the development and transformation of "western rationality" as the activities that gave rise to the natural sciences. (I shall return to Foucault's treatment of this notion later when we explore the use that Hardt and Negri make of Foucault's linked conception of "biopower".)

The salient feature of *Empire* as principle of intelligibility that I wish to focus on is found in the following passage (which I have already quoted above):

Empire presents itself not as a historical regime originating in conquest, but rather as an order *that effectively suspends history* [my emphasis] and thereby fixes the existing state of affairs for eternity. From the perspective of Empire, this is the way things will always be and the way they were always meant to be. In other words, Empire presents its rule not as a transitory moment *in the movement of history* [my emphasis] but as a regime with no temporal boundaries, and in this sense outside of history or at the end of history.

What Hardt and Negri want us to see is that there is indeed in the world today something that can be intelligibly called "Empire," whose purpose is to consolidate its form of rule as a "New World Order," an order that is finally able to achieve the peace and prosperity that human beings have always wished for, and that today can only be envisaged on a global scale. However, by showing that Empire actually proceeds by a consolidated effort to establish such a form of rule, Hardt and Negri at the same time point to the forces that this form of rule intends effectively to rule. Like Marx and Engels, Hardt and Negri show that, at least as far as our world is presently organized, we need to distinguish between, on the one hand, the forms and structures of that organization, and who controls in the name of what, and, on the other hand, the forces that actually get organized in the particular ways that they do.

If we are to relate this general point to our individual lives as they unfold from day to day, it is the distinction between, on the one hand, what and how I do what I do every day, and, on the other hand, the fact that I am the one who does it. Whatever part I may have in deciding what and how I do what I do on a given day, which may be considerable or may be negligible, the point of the distinction is to remind us that it will not get done unless I do it, or someone else does it. It is important not to allow ourselves to downplay the fundamental, indeed, ontological point being made here by recognizing that it is not necessary that I do x or y, because if I do not do it, someone else will. If I do not do it, someone else *must* do it, *if* x or y is to get done. X or y will not *be* if it does not get done by the likes of you and me. I insist on these elementary points to compensate for the "cog in the machine" feeling that many of us, if not most of us, feel about the nature and extent of our contribution to the social forms that make up the world. The "forms" would not "function" if they were not made to function by the expenditure of our efforts to live out our lives in that world. The "forms" of the world depend on our physical, corporeal, breathing-in-and-out engagement *in* the world.

The means and forms of particular productive capacities of a given society depend on the productive forces of that society, and the productive forces of any society, the expenditures of energy they represent, are the animating movement of that society, the breathing in-and-out, bodily displacements of beings establishing and maintaining relations with each other. What Hardt and Negri want us to see is that the animating movement of social life today has taken on decidedly "immaterial" forms, in a way that allows us to see the dynamic of the basic struggle identified by Marx and Engels in a new light. Today, while most of us are still required to make a living—that is, to have most of our daily activities constrained by the obtaining and exchange of money for products we make use of, or consume—more and more of us make that living less by producing "material" objects or commodities than by producing "immaterial" ones, the examples that Hardt and Negri give being (*Empire*, p. 290) "a service, a cultural product, knowledge, or communication." Specifically, they include increased engagement in what Hardt and Negri call (*Multitude*, p. 108) "affective labour," that is, "labour that produces or manipulates affects, such as feelings of ease, well-being, satisfaction, excitement, or passion," as, for instance, "in the work of legal assistants, flight attendants, and fast food workers (service with a smile)."

These observations allow us to see differently, and call upon us to theorize differently, the dynamic that animates social life. Hardt and Negri describe the difference in the following way (*Multitude*, p. 146):

> Material production—the production, for example, of cars, televisions, clothing, and food—creates the *means of social life*. Modern forms of social life would not be possible without these commodities. Immaterial production, by contrast, including the production of ideas, images, knowledges, communication, cooperation, and affective relations, tends to create not the means of social life but *social life itself*. Immaterial production is biopolitical.

It is by means of the term "biopolitical" that Hardt and Negri seek to redescribe the dynamics at the heart of the basic struggle that animates contemporary social life. According to Hardt and Negri, if Marx was able to describe a basic struggle shaping itself into an opposition between the bourgeoisie's ownership of the means of production and the productive forces of the proletariat itself, today that struggle needs to be understood less in terms of a dialectically tense confrontation than as animating a "collective biopolitical body," which cannot be neatly divided into "base" and "superstructure." What Hardt and Negri want us to notice (*Empire*, p. 30) is that this

> body becomes structure not by negating the originary productive force that animates it but by recognizing it; it becomes language (both scientific and social language) because it is a multitude of singular and determinate bodies that seek relation. It is thus both production and reproduction, structure and superstructure, because it is life in the fullest sense and politics in the proper sense. Our analysis has to descend

into the jungle of productive and conflictual determinations that the collective biopolitical body offers us. The context of our analysis thus has to be the very unfolding of life itself, the process of the constitution of the world, of history. The analysis must be proposed not through ideal forms but within the dense complex of experience.

What Hardt and Negri propose to help us make our way through this "dense complex of experience" is a rearticulation of the terms of the struggle we are engaged in, a struggle against "biopower" in the name of the possibilities inherent in "biopolitical production."

The distinction between "biopower" and "biopolitics" that Hardt and Negri make use of tracks the distinction they make between Empire and multitude. If we understand these terms as "principles of intelligibility" that help us make sense of the movement that animates our changing world—principles that make use of, but also compete with, other notions, such as "globalization" or "postmodernity," which also contain an implicit sense of what I have been calling the "movement" of history—then the notion of "biopower" is meant to describe the different ways in which Empire consolidates its hold on the forces of production, which Hardt and Negri further distinguish in terms of "immaterial" production and "affective labour," or, more generally, "biopolitical" production. The productive forces within the "biopolitical" are theorized as generating a "biopolitics" that is meant to capture and make sense of the movement of the multitude, which, in its resistance to "biopower," gradually reveals itself as a "power-to" produce a "commonality" that challenges the reactionary rule of biopower. Stated more succinctly, "biopower" is what imperial sovereignty or Empire exercises as a "power-over" the forces of social production of the multitude, which itself is becoming increasingly "biopolitical" through the development of "immaterial labour."

A good way to keep these two forms of power distinct is to think of constituted power as "power-over" the forces exhibited by the constituting "power-to" of human energies and efforts. This "power-over" is accomplished through the structural organization of those energies and efforts. (We shall come back to this particular way of describing the distinction a little later.) As Hardt and Negri explain (*Multitude*, pp. 94–95):

> In such immaterial labour, production spills over beyond the bounds of the economy traditionally conceived to engage culture, society, and politics directly. What is produced in this case is not just material goods but actual social relationships and forms of life. We will call this kind of production "biopolitical" to highlight how general its products are and how directly it engages in its entirety.

It is this engagement of life "in its entirety" that calls for the prefix "bio-" in both "biopower" and "biopolitics," but Hardt and Negri want to show that the engagements are quite different: "Biopower stands above society, transcendent, as a sovereign authority and imposes its order. Biopolitical production, in contrast, is immanent to society and creates social relationships and forms through collaborative forms of labour." Or, as they put the point in *Empire* (p. 62):

> From one perspective Empire stands clearly over the multitude and subjects it to
> the rule of its overarching machine, as a new Leviathan. At the same time, however,
> from the perspective of social productivity and creativity, from what we have been
> calling the ontological perspective, the hierarchy is reversed. The multitude is the real
> productive force of our social world, whereas Empire is a mere apparatus of capture
> that lives only off the vitality of the multitude—as Marx would say, a vampire regime
> of accumulated dead labour that survives only by sucking off the blood of the living.

The key expression of the dynamics of the struggle between Empire and the multitude is captured in the way in which Hardt and Negri seek to demonstrate how, despite the basic contours of the struggle (*Multitude*, p. 225), "Empire and the multitude are not symmetrical: whereas Empire is constantly dependent on the multitude and its social productivity, the multitude is *potentially autonomous* [my emphasis] and has the capacity to create society on its own." It is precisely the "potential autonomy" of the movement of the multitude that will be the focus of the remainder of this chapter. It is here that I think we can best respond to the question of where we are headed, give more substance to the sense that the world is becoming increasingly multicultural, and show how these two matters that concern us are indeed connected, in a way that can renew our hope and confidence in the future.

When we note that the world is becoming increasingly multicultural we are noting that it is changing. A changing world is disconcerting for some, including, normally, those who are comfortable with the world as it is. Yet, if history teaches us anything, it teaches us that the world is always changing. The study of history tracks those changes by reconstructing the movement of historical change, the ways in which it has engendered and destroyed various developments as these have been manifested in the ways in which human beings relate to one another. When we place ourselves within history we are placing ourselves within these developmental movements. We can speak of history as a whole as movement, but that is a very general statement. When we look more closely at this general movement we discern any number of various developments working themselves out. We can then try and make sense of the ways in which these developments are working themselves out, which of course is a particular way of participating in them.

If, then, we place ourselves within a changing world that shows itself as becoming increasingly multicultural, we are placing ourselves within particular developmental movements. One of the most obvious and most concrete ways of understanding the movements that render our world increasingly multicultural is to consider the migratory movements of people as they uproot and displace themselves in order to remake their lives elsewhere. Hardt and Negri allow us to theorize this movement, not from the perspective of the various destinations that receive "immigrants," but from the movement itself, in the desire for better lives. As they write (*Multitude*, p. 133):

> Part of the wealth of migrants is their desire for something more, their refusal to accept the way things are. Certainly, most migrations are driven by the need to escape conditions of violence, starvation, or deprivation, but together with that negative condition there is also the positive desire for wealth, peace, and freedom. *This combined act of refusal and expression of desire is enormously powerful* [my emphasis].

Indeed, I would like to argue that in an increasingly multicultural world—that is, one that understands that history is moving us in the direction of increasing interaction between people from different backgrounds—it is becoming clearer how our anticipations are best represented by this "combined act of refusal" to accept the world as it is presently organized and "expression of desire" for a better world, one that recognizes that a shared world is a world that combines the many possibilities of different worlds into a "common" world. Again, as Hardt and Negri point out (*Multitude*, p. 133): "Migrants may often travel empty-handed in conditions of extreme poverty, but even then they are full of knowledges, languages, skills, and creative capacities: each migrant brings with him or her an entire world." An increasingly multicultural world increasingly recognizes the importance and wealth of what migrants carry with(in) them. Of course, the focus is still too often on the "contribution" that can be made to some established order, for example, a receiving state as defined by its immigration policies. However, rather than focus on the "reception" of "immigrants" into the relative ordering of particular nation-states, if one focuses on the movement itself, which is propelled by both refusal and desire, one can discern a very different world, not a constituted world, but one that is being constituted through the affirmation of the differences of its singular capacities.

This is not to say that nation-states are obsolete within the new imperial order. On the contrary, according to Hardt and Negri (*Empire*, p. 310), they still serve various functions: political mediation with respect to the transnational corporations, and redistribution of income according to biopolitical needs within their own limited territories. Nation-states are filters of the flow of global circulation and regulators of the articulation of global command; in other words, they capture and distribute the flows of wealth to and from the global power, and they discipline their own populations as much as this is still possible.

Nevertheless, tracking this movement is tracking the movement of what Hardt and Negri theorize as "the multitude," a term that allows us to move away from the adjective "multicultural," which too often constrains us merely to qualify an existing social order in terms of its always limited recognition of differences. What needs to be understood is that, in the current developing movement of history, it is the representatives of these different social orders that are constrained to respond to the affirmations of forces they cannot do without, forces that increasingly affirm themselves as singularities (*Empire*, p. 395):

> The multitude affirms its singularity by inverting the ideological illusion that all humans on the global surfaces of the world market are interchangeable. Standing the ideology of the market on its feet, the multitude promotes through its labour the biopolitical singularizations of groups and sets of humanity, across each and every node of global interchange.

What Hardt and Negri are sketching, it seems to me, is a coherent way to make sense of what I discussed in the Introduction of this book, namely, how to think the fact that our increasingly multicultural world is both a *multi*cultural world and *one* world. We can do so if we shift our focus from the interaction of different cultures to the formation of a mode of coming together through our desire to share our different capacities. Note that this coming together is not one that asks of the participants that they abandon their singularities. On the contrary, it is because we are all singularities that we seek one another out, in order to share what those singularities have to offer. "The multitude" is precisely meant to denote this active seeking out and sharing. "The multitude" describes the movement and formation of itself as a whole composed of what Hardt and Negri call (*Multitude*, p. 105) "singularities that act in common."

This movement is perhaps best expressed in the unruly forces that resist and challenge the forms of rule that seek to consolidate privileged positions within the "New World Order," the rule of imperial network power. It is these unruly forces that the concept of "multitude" is meant to express and ultimately to help construct as a counterimperial force. More than that, Hardt and Negri also assert (*Multitude*, p. 219) that "the multitude provides us with a social subject and a logic of social organization that make possible today, for the very first time, the realization of democracy."

What needs to be done, that is, what needs to be theorized, is not an alternative form of rule, but that which poses itself as the challenge to any form of rule as a "power-over" that finds its most complete expression in the rule of Empire. In other words, what needs to be theorized is the productive potential of the unruly forces themselves. Hence the project of articulating this potential through the concept of "multitude."

One way of doing this is by distinguishing "the multitude" from "the masses" or "the mob." The latter display an unruliness as well, but it is one that does not belong to any project and consequently they are prone to manipulation. The unruliness of the multitude, on the other hand, is precisely one that can be theorized. This is done by appealing to the notion of singularities and defining "the multitude" as a set of singularities by which is designated (*Multitude*, p. 99) "a social subject whose difference cannot be reduced to sameness, a difference that remains different." It is this dimension of social subjectivity that theoretically distinguishes the multitude from crowds, masses and mobs. As Hardt and Negri write (*Multitude*, p. 100):

> Since the different individuals or groups that make up the crowd are incoherent and recognize no common shared elements, their collection of differences remains inert and can easily appear as one indifferent aggregate. The components of the masses, the mob, and the crowd are not singularities—and this is obvious from the fact that their differences so easily collapse into the indifference of the whole. Moreover, these social subjects are fundamentally passive, in the sense that they cannot act by themselves but rather must be led. The crowd or the mob or the rabble can have social effects— often horribly destructive effects—but cannot act of their own accord. That is why they are so susceptible to external manipulation. The multitude designates an active social subject, which acts on the basis of what the singularities share in common. The multitude is an internally different, multiple social subject, whose constitution and action is based not on identity or unity (or, much less, indifference) but on what it has in common.

To get a sense of what Hardt and Negri are talking about, and attempting to theorize, one need only think of participation in a large protest march. A protest march is an activity of "the multitude," something particularly manifest when it is large, filling city streets, describing a completely different circulating flow than the usual one even when it respects certain rules, such as marching the right way down a highway, while overriding others, by, for instance, not stopping at red lights. The march, although it gathers numerous people, is not a crowd. Crowds gather around objects other than themselves, but a march gathers around itself. It thus makes sense to call it a "subject," but it is a multiple subject. The gathering that a protest march initiates is variously justified for the participants. Although it may have a focus or target, the commonalities that it expresses are not reduced or restricted to them. Although it has organizers, it is not a function of that organization. Indeed, it might be said that the reason why it has organizers is because it is a self-generating activity that, in that self-generation, calls for organization and thus organizers. A protest march is both movement and expression, usually culminating at a particular spot where various speeches are heard, although, interestingly, those speeches often prove to be anticlimactic, usually because the speakers try too hard to rally around particular conceptions and interests what has already been self-constituted through the march. The speeches continue that self-constitution when they are explicitly celebratory rather than moralistic.

Thus, as this example illustrates, the action of the multitude is real, but it is also ideal. As Foucault tells us, that is what we should expect from a principle of intelligibility, in the sense that a principle of intelligibility, while it regulates what is thought about the real, also, at the same time as it is formulated, increasingly prescribes an ideal. That is, the function of making sense of a given reality is supplemented by the task of giving sense or direction to the modes of thinking that it governs and regulates. If one treats Hardt and Negri's conception of Empire/multitude as a principle of intelligibility, that is, as something that is meant to allow us to make sense of features of the world that are not well-served by existing and established modes of thought, then I think it becomes an interesting attempt to capture the sense of movement within social life that many simply call "history."

One might propose as a definition of "history" precisely this sense of the movement of social life as the realities that it confronts struggle with the ideals that it espouses. One should note the profoundly historical dimension to Hardt and Negri's theorizing, the fact that they see themselves as participating in a wider process to which they wish to contribute in part by attempting to articulate the telos of this historical process, which they call (*Empire*, p. 395) the material affirmation of the liberation of the multitude. The affirmation is material, and therefore real, but its reality takes the form of an affirmation, and in that sense is ideal. As Hardt and Negri write (*Empire*, p. 296):

> The teleology of the multitude is theurgical; it consists in the possibility of directing technologies and production toward its own joy and its own increase in power.
> The multitude has no reason to look outside its own history and its own present productive power for the means necessary to lead toward its constitution as a political subject.

It seems to me that when we look up from our texts, and consider and engage our increasingly multicultural world, we can in effect see ourselves as participating in this movement of history. That is, when we recognize that the world is increasingly becoming multicultural we are implicitly recognizing and acknowledging that, as Hardt and Negri put it (*Multitude*, p. 127), "we are a multiplicity of singular forms of life and *at the same time* share a common global existence." Such recognition and acknowledgement call upon us (*Multitude*, p. 126) to "think all cultural singularities not as anachronistic survivals of the past but as equal participants in our common present." This common present lived in contact—the function of the present within the past-present-future complex called history—leads us to articulate our shared anticipations of the future, anticipations shaped through the "cooperation, collaboration, and communication" that shapes what Hardt and Negri theorize as "the common." As they insist (*Multitude*, p. 128):

> Once we recognize singularity, the common begins to emerge. Singularities do communicate, and they are able to do so because of the common they share. We share bodies with two eyes, ten fingers, ten toes; we share life on this Earth; we share capitalist regimes of production and exploitation; we share common dreams of a better future. Our communication, collaboration, and cooperation, furthermore, not only are based on the common that exists, but also in turn produce the common. We make and remake the common we share every day.

"The common we share every day" is the world we engage every day, not a theoretical world but a real/ideal world produced through our interaction with one another on a daily basis, at work, during our leisure activities, in our attempts to live better lives. It is this creation of the common that best describes our "living labour," which Hardt and Negri, following Marx, describe (*Multitude*, p. 146) as "the fundamental human faculty: the ability to engage the world actively and create social life." This common is increasingly created through our increasing engagement in forms of immaterial labour, which, even if they are still largely controlled by imperial rule through different processes of private appropriation, nevertheless points beyond the dictates of imperial rule. The continued exploitation of our immaterial labour is at the same time the exploitation of our continued ability to speak to one another, and this ability to speak to one another is precisely what enables us to create the common we share. As Hardt and Negri insist (*Multitude*, p. 201):

> our power to speak is based in the common, that is, our shared language; every linguistic act creates the common; and the act of speech itself is conducted in

common, in dialogue, in communication. This triple relation to the common illustrated by language characterizes immaterial labour.

In an increasingly multicultural world our shared languages can no longer be conceived as a single language, as a mother tongue or a national language. Rather, language, like speech, needs to be understood in the mode of communication, of communicating with one another, which increasingly defines what we do anyway through our biopolitical productivity. The task at hand is to redirect that productivity away from the controlled interest of the few to the common interest, which (*Multitude*, p. 206) "is a general interest that is not made abstract in the control of the state, but rather reappropriated by the singularities that cooperate in social, biopolitical production; it is a public interest not in the hands of a bureaucracy, but managed democratically by the multitude." Such democratic "management" itself needs to be modelled on the mode of communication (*Multitude*, p. 211):

> In political organization as in narration, there is a constant dialogue among diverse, singular subjects, a polyphonic composition of them, and a general enrichment of each through this common constitution. The multitude in movement is a kind of narration that produces new subjectivities and new languages.

The appeal to democracy here can be seen as an appeal to Balibar's "ideal universality," the principle of "equaliberty" that describes both the movement or dynamics of history *and* its end or telos, which can no longer be denied. Evoking the universal appeal to some concept of democracy by various forms of rule, Hardt and Negri insist that (*Multitude*, p. 220):

> Democracy can no longer be evaluated in the liberal manner, as a limit of equality, or in the socialist way, as a limit of freedom, but rather must be the radicalization without reserve of both freedom and equality. Perhaps some day soon we will have arrived at the point when we can look back with irony at the barbaric old times when in order to be free we had to keep our brothers and sisters slaves, or to be equal we were constrained to inhuman sacrifices of freedom. In our view, freedom and equality can be the motors of a revolutionary reinvention of democracy.

That revolutionary potential is to be found in "the multitude," Hardt and Negri's equivalent to Marx's proletariat, given that, in their view (*Empire*, p. 237), "Having achieved the global level, capitalist development is faced directly with the multitude, without mediation." The multitude, through the dynamics of its engagement in immaterial, communicative labour, is finally able to articulate the telos of its effort, which is that same immaterial, communicative working together to develop our various capacities that moves us beyond the need to be ruled through fear, the hallmark of biopower, in order to celebrate the desire for life that animates the common world we share.

The Dynamic Telos of History: A Shared Democratic World

I have sought in this book to make the case that speculative philosophy of history can help us better respond to the question of where we are headed. The case needs to be made, in my view, because we all have a sense that we are headed somewhere, although we tend, today, to be unacceptably inarticulate about where that is. I say "unacceptably inarticulate" because more and more of us live the kinds of lives that include the ability, the time, and the inclination to *think* about this question. Of course, it is to such people that this book is addressed, given that you are the ones likely to read it.

Besides, many of us do have a sense of where we are headed that, if pressed, we might express in one of the following ways. Some of us would say that we are headed toward disaster, or, more generally and less dramatically, towards a future that is worse than the present. Others would say that we are headed, or can be headed if we try to coordinate more of our efforts, towards a better world, or towards a future that is better than the present, with less injustice, less poverty, less conflict or, at least, better mechanisms for resolving conflicts. Still others would say that we are headed, as we always have been and always will be, toward more of the same, a mixture of good and bad, pain and pleasure, happiness and despair.

I think that we can do better. One of the points I would like to insist on in this conclusion is that the more we think and talk about the question of where we are headed, the better sense we will have, not only of *where* we are headed, but of the fact that we are headed there *together*.

The sense of where we are headed and the realization that we are headed there together are linked to what I have called throughout this book the telos of history and the dynamics of history, notions that are primary concerns for speculative philosophy of history. Such a philosophy is "speculative" because it is dealing with a whole of which it cannot claim any knowledge, for the simple reason that the philosophical attempt to make sense of the whole forms part of that developing whole itself. We do not experience the whole as such, we participate *in* it. Our sense of it is a participatory one. It includes knowledge of parts of it, but it also includes hopes and expectations, and an openness to what it has yet to reveal.

There are different ways to characterize the whole within which we participate. The way that I have been privileging is treating it as *history*, because it seems to me that, if we are to try to respond seriously to this question of where we are headed, then we need to think about how the future—where we are headed—links to its logically dependent notions of the present and the past. This, of course, is why I have called history "the past-present-future complex."

The logical interdependence of these three notions—the past, the present, and the future—is not as easy to put into words as one might think, even though we live that interdependence every day of our lives. For every today there is a yesterday and a tomorrow. Indeed, any attempt, my own included, to put it into words needs to be tested against the everyday living out of our lives. What I would like to do in this conclusion is run my own test of what I have written and argued here against the living out of the life that I live and share with the reader. I shall do so by summing up how the telos and the dynamics of history work within the frameworks proposed by our three speculative philosophers of history—Kant, Hegel, Marx—with specific reference to my understanding of how we are currently living out our lives.

Kant, like most of us, thinks that we do the best we can with what we have and try to make the most of it. However, Kant the philosopher does not restrict himself to considering things from this individual perspective. If we move up from the individual level to the social level, the best that we can do individually is certainly not very good, precisely because the individual interests of each of us tend to conflict with those of others. Social life becomes the scene of generalized conflict between conflicting interests. Those conflicts can be destructive, especially when they escalate into warfare. Kant argues, however, that, if we take a longer, historical view of social life, other factors become apparent, namely, human rationality and ingenuity. From the perspective of the longer, historical view, the incessant conflict displayed at the social level has *over time* come to manifest itself in more productive ways, including the development of institutions designed to mediate those social conflicts. Thus, for Kant, from the perspective of history, or as he himself puts it, from the perspective of a "universal history from a cosmopolitan point of view," what appears at the social level to be incessant conflict can be seen as a kind of "unsocial sociability," which promotes the development of our natural capacities as human beings.

For Kant, then, the dynamics of history stem from our own particular striving. Such striving lands us into conflicts with others, where, of course, there are winners and losers, but these conflicts themselves have been occasions for the development of our natural faculties, which, if they had not been stimulated by such conflictual situations, would have remained undeveloped.

We are all familiar with the idea that competitive situations tend to demand of people greater efforts than they might otherwise devote to a given activity. These greater efforts produce greater results, results that themselves may not have been intended but from which we benefit—"we" being understood here as human beings generally. I see no point in denying that this is true in many different kinds of cases and situations. Conflict and competition are indeed productive. I will even grant Kant the notion that such productive conflict and competition drive the development of our social lives, and structure a good portion of our individual lives, especially that portion that is devoted to making a living.

So far, Kant's speculative considerations concerning the dynamics of the historical process pass the test of relating in a concrete way to our lived experience. Large parts of our lives are indeed built around a kind of "unsocial sociability," focused on self-interest but mitigated by a more or less grudging respect for the self-interest that belongs to others.

From consideration of these dynamics within the context of *historical* development, which of course means a context that extends beyond the bounds of explicit and restricted self-interest, Kant speculates about the telos or direction of the "unsocial sociability" of our interactions. The long-term, historical development of human conflict reveals a perfecting of human capacities that allows one to imagine, that is, to speculate about, an end or telos of fully developed human capacities. This, too, can be said to reflect itself in our lives, insofar as we commit to developing our natural capacities, both in ourselves considered individually and in others considered socially. We build schools—public and private, professional, vocational, occasional, specialized—and we develop sporting venues and health clubs, indeed clubs of all kinds catering to different abilities and capacities that we discover ourselves to possess or desire to possess. When considering all of this activity, especially with regard to its focused nature—all these activities aim at something—it makes sense to consider whether or not all of it might be contributing to an identifiable overall end. Kant's merit is to have us think about that end as an *ideal*, which, even if it is not, and indeed, for Kant, cannot, be fully realized within our particular lives, can nevertheless serve as a guide to how best to pursue those activities. It provides an ultimate framework within which those activities can be evaluated. It allows us to ask to what extent the activities and institutions that we participate in actually structure and promote the *full* development of our natural faculties and abilities.

However, as I have already argued in this book, the problem with Kant's account is that his conception of the conflictual dynamics that animate social life is in fact too *disconnected* from the telos of the full development of our natural capacities. That is, there does not seem to be a sufficiently clear *historical* connection between the dynamics that animate social life and the ideal that provides its ultimate direction. Kant thinks that the ultimate direction is provided by "Nature," with history being merely the unfolding of Nature's "secret plan," but where does that leave our own concrete efforts to realize our natural faculties? It leaves them precisely where Kant locates them, in a conflictual social situation of competing self-interests. From the perspective that places itself *within* that conflictual social situation, the telos seems very far off indeed. In fact, it is infinitely far off, because it describes an asymptotic ideal.

Yet is it really so very far off? Or rather, is the full development of our "natural" faculties and abilities equally far off for everyone, or does our *actual* conflictual social situation not provide for the development of *some* at the expense of others? Do not the institutions and other social structures that have developed, in order to mitigate the destructive effects of social conflict and to promote its productive potentials, favour the development of some at the expense of others? In other words, does not consideration of Kant's particular conception of history reveal that it is not so much *self*-interest that animates our conflictual social situation as the consolidation and promotion of *some* interests at the expense of others, as, for example, in the creation of wealth for some at the expense of health of those who actually produce it? The dynamics of our particular conflictual social situation are not the result of some abstract conception of self-interest, but rather the result of the promotion of the self-interest of *some* at the expense of the self-interest of others. Concretely, this translates into particular opportunities and the conditions of their availability within the social situation that we find ourselves in, such as entrance requirements for different schools, including fees and various qualifications. It appears that the telos of the full development of our natural capacities is not *equally* "infinitely" far off, after all, which renders its asymptotic status highly questionable.

In other words, a closer look at the historically specific dimensions of the dynamics of conflict shows, not an abstract picture of competing self-interests, but specific conflicts generated by the particular (historically specific) structures of the social situation, structures that are maintained by some and contested by others, as in disputes, for example, over the funding and administration of education or health care. To put it more simply, the dynamics of *historical* social life are not best described by "conflict" in the singular, but by "conflicts" in the plural, insofar as these describe the unequal conditions maintained by particular social structures.

This simple putting of "conflict" into the plural requires that we radically revise our conception of the connection between the dynamics of history and the telos of history. If the dynamics that animate history are *particular* conflicts, that means that they are to be understood, not in terms of some general principle such as self-interest, but in terms of their own specific characteristics.

The question we need to ask is: what makes a particular conflict *particular*? The answer is interesting: the particularity of a conflict is largely defined by the particular way in which it includes the terms of its own resolution. Conflicts in this sense differ from one another in terms of the resolutions that they call for. That is, it is the resolutions that define the conflicts as the particular conflicts that they are. Let us take, as an example, the Israeli–Palestinian conflict, the possible resolution of which is described by Todd May, in an interview with Jason Adams in April 2005, in the following way:

> Israel needs to remove itself to the 1967 borders, that is to say, to end the occupation. In addition, some negotiated recognition of the right of return must be established. To those who say that Israeli settlement activity has gone too far to allow such a return, I say that the solution then would be a single state where Jews and Palestinians enjoy equal political status.

The conflict continues *because* the actions required to effect a resolution are not being taken by those in a position to take them, for any number of reasons (the examination of which is beyond the scope of the present discussion). Meanwhile, other actions are being taken in response to the very failure to take those actions, but those other actions serve only to exacerbate the conflict, without changing the terms of its possible resolution. Therefore the conflict endures. Nevertheless, such conflicts, when viewed *historically*, do not endure indefinitely, which is another way of saying that they are particular.

Interestingly, from the historical point of view, conflicts do not end because they are finally resolved within the terms that define them, but because they are *transformed* by unexpected circumstances and give way to new circumstances. Thus we have historical *change*. Hegel's speculative philosophy of history attempts to grasp the direction of this change by examining the unfolding of these transformations. The fact that Hegel reads these historical changes *as* transformations allows him to speculate about the aim or goal of history itself as a transformative process. That aim or goal, according to Hegel, is the transformative realization of reason within the world, effected through the particular conflicts that are generated in social life through our passionate engagements with and against each other.

If we set Hegel against Kant, we find that the dynamics of social life are animated, not by an abstract "unsocial sociability," but by the various struggles for *mutual recognition* that underlie our passionate engagements. It is through the mutuality of recognition that defines social life, including its dysfunctional forms of *mis*recognition and *non*-recognition, that our passionate engagements are transformed into spaces of "reason-ability," which increasingly mediate our interactions.

Again in contrast with Kant, Hegel allows us to understand more clearly the dynamics of social life, which are not merely conflicts generated by self-interest, but particular conflicts that have their own ways of structuring the relations that we establish with each other through our passionate engagements. These dynamics can also be seen to yield precisely those spaces of "reason-ability" that allow us to develop our capacities and abilities in ways we would have been unable to develop independently of them.

I think that Hegel's speculative considerations throw interesting light on our increasingly multicultural world. Our world is increasingly "multicultural" in the sense that a variety of people of different cultural backgrounds increasingly live in contact with one another, thus creating a particular kind of social space. A key feature of this social space, I have argued, is the recognition by those who live within it, not only that it is structured by both the familiar and unfamiliar—the familiar developed within one's family contact, the unfamiliar resulting from also being in contact with an extra-familial world—but that it comprises *unfamiliar familiarities*, different ways of making sense of the world. Recognition of these unfamiliar familiarities as forming part of a shared social space cannot but modulate the passionate engagement of each of us with others. Indeed, this modulation through the dynamics of mutual recognition speaks to the fact, or rather the movement expressed by the fact, that our world is indeed becoming increasingly multicultural. Our passionate engagements increasingly demand that we recognize each other in and through our engagements, that is, within the spaces of "reason-ability" created by the attempt to establish relations based on mutuality.

In the multicultural spaces of most Western democracies these demands for mutual recognition usually get expressed in terms of the recognition of rights, sometimes constitutionally guaranteed within given state structures, sometimes appealed to from a moral point of view. Thus, through Hegel, we see how from the dynamics of history—the struggle for mutual recognition creating a shared social space of "reason-ability"—a telos of *universality* arises or emerges. The universal arises or emerges out of the struggle for mutuality because the latter requires of us, as John Russon might put it, a self-transcending critique of our supposed self-interest. This is reflected in the sense that most of us have that, despite our differences, and indeed *because* of those differences, our world is increasingly one that we are called upon to share.

However, as Marx has helped us notice, this universality of mutual recognition, and the spaces of "reason-ability" that it creates and sustains, are hardly equally distributed across the various populations of the planet. In fact, more often than not, they seem to be the privilege only of the privileged. Too many people inhabit, not spaces of "reason-ability," but spaces of bodily exploitation that leave little room for mutuality. It seems that, on Hegel's view of history, ultimately, as long as spaces of "reason-ability" are created and sustained, then that is sufficient to enable us to say that the telos is realizing itself, even if many people, not to say most, do not live out their lives within those spaces, and their lives are summed up as passions spent rather than reason realized.

For Marx, it is not the "idea of freedom" that needs to prevail in history, but the free development of each and therefore of all. The dynamics of history for Marx are not first and foremost a struggle for *recognition*. Rather, history is fuelled by the living labour of all of us, our combined productive forces. We are unfree insofar as the productive forces, to which we each contribute most of our waking lives, are exploited in the interests of *some* rather than in the interests of the productive forces themselves, our lives being given over to the enrichment of some in exchange for a (standard of) living. Although, like Hegel, Marx sees in *mutuality* the true movement of history, the direction that it sets itself as it struggles with those consolidated powers of vested interest; the telos of history for Marx is a world other than one controlled in the interests of a few, a world that reflects the interests of all as these express themselves in our passionately *mutual* engagements with one another, understood now not principally as conflictual but as associative, *within* which conflicts will no doubt arise but need not overwhelm.

This world is our actual world, not a dream world. It is the world that arises out of our daily interactions, governed by an everyday "*social* sociability," wherever we are called to engage with one another, at work, in our families and neighbourhoods, in our travels and projects. It is a world greatly enriched by the differences that many cultures, many singularities, can provide in, as Hardt and Negri put it, "communication, collaboration, and cooperation," and that can provide for the continued development and creation of our individual and combined capacities.

In the end the best way to evaluate these speculative attempts to make sense of history, through an understanding of its dynamics and its telos, might be to see which one best fits the modal square within which our lives unfold.

Which attempt allows us to assume our contingent presence on Earth, through acknowledgement of the necessities that have contributed to the present structures of the world, but with a strong sense of its possibilities, limited only by the impossible? In my view Marx's insistence on a dynamics of living labour, devoted to a telos of the free development of each and therefore of all, is the most successful. It conceives the necessities of past exploitation as structuring a contingent relation to the present that can be transformed by focusing on the real possibility of living and working together in ways that not only develop our natural capacities as productive and creative forces, but make it impossible for us to ignore the freedom and equality that attention to the struggles of history shows belong to us all.

Works Cited

Adams, Jason. (2005, April 12). "Interview with Todd May" [online]. www.livejournal. com/community/siyahi/1572 [consulted September 10, 2007].

Angus, Ian. (2004). "Empire, Borders, Place: A Critique of Hardt and Negri's Concept of Empire." *Theory and Event* 7:3.

Appiah, Kwame Anthony. (2006). *Cosmopolitanism: Ethics in a World of Strangers.* New York: W. W. Norton.

Balibar, Étienne. (1995). "Ambiguous Universality." *Differences: A Journal of Feminist Cultural Studies* 7:1.

Brandom, Robert B. (1994). *Making It Explicit: Reasoning, Representing, and Discursive Commitment.* Cambridge, MA: Harvard University Press.

Brookner, Anita. (2005). *Leaving Home.* London: Viking.

Calhoun, Craig. (2002, Fall). "The Class Consciousness of Frequent Travelers: Toward a Critique of Actually Existing Cosmopolitanism." *South Atlantic Quarterly* 101:4.

Connolly, William E. (1993). *The Terms of Political Discourse.* Princeton, NJ: Princeton University Press.

Connolly, William E. (2002). *Neuropolitics: Thinking, Culture, Speed.* Minneapolis: University of Minnesota Press.

Derrida, Jacques. (2000, December). "Hospitality." *Angelaki: Journal of the Theoretical Humanities* 5:3.

Descartes, René. (1993). *Meditations on First Philosophy* [1642], trans. Donald A. Cress. Indianapolis, IN: Hackett.

Diamond, Jared. (2005). *Collapse: How Societies Choose to Fail or Succeed.* New York: Viking.

Duby, Georges. (1992). "Foreword," in Philippe Ariès and Georges Duby (general editors). *A History of Private Life*, Volume 1, *From Pagan Rome to Byzantium*, trans. Arthur Goldhammer. Cambridge, MA: Belknap Press of Harvard University Press.

Fillion, Réal. (1991). "Realizing Reason in History: How Cunning Does It Have To Be?" *The Owl of Minerva* 23:1.

Fillion, Réal. (2005). "Moving Beyond Biopower: Hardt and Negri's Post-Foucauldian Speculative Philosophy of History." *History and Theory* 44:4.

Foucault, Michel. (1998). "Nietzsche, Genealogy, History" [1977], in *Essential Works of Foucault, 1954–1984*, Volume 2, *Aesthetics, Method, and Epistemology*, ed. James D. Faubion. New York: New Press.

Foucault, Michel. (2004). *Sécurité, Territoire, Population: Cours au Collège de France, 1977–1978*. Paris: Seuil/Gallimard.

Fukuyama, Francis. (1992). *The End of History and The Last Man*. New York: Free Press.

Gardner, Howard. (1993). *Frames of Mind: The Theory of Multiple Intelligences*. New York: Basic.

Hampshire, Stuart. (1999). *Justice is Conflict*. Princeton, NJ: Princeton University Press.

Hardt, Michael, and Antonio Negri. (2000). *Empire*. Cambridge, MA: Harvard University Press.

Hardt, Michael, and Antonio Negri. (2004). *Multitude: War in the Age of Empire*. New York: Penguin Press.

Hegel, Georg Wilhelm Friedrich (1975). *Lectures on the Philosophy of World History: Introduction, Reason in History* [1837], trans. H. B. Nisbet. Cambridge and New York: Cambridge University Press.

Held, David. (2004). "Democratic Accountability and Political Effectiveness from a Cosmopolitan Perspective." *Government and Opposition* 39: 2.

Hobsbawm, E. J. (1962). *The Age of Revolution: 1789–1848*. New York: New American Library.

Honneth, Axel. (1997). "Is Universalism a Moral Trap? The Presuppositions and Limits of Human Rights," in James Bohman and Matthias Lutz-Bachmann (ed.), *Perpetual Peace: Essays on Kant's Cosmopolitan Ideal*. Cambridge, MA: MIT Press.

Huntington, Samuel P. (1996). *The Clash of Civilizations and the Remaking of World Order*. New York: Touchstone.

Kant, Immanuel. (1963). "Idea for a Universal History from a Cosmopolitan Point of View" [1784] and "Perpetual Peace" [1795], trans. Lewis White Beck, in *On History*, ed. Lewis White Beck. Indianapolis, IN: Bobbs–Merrill.

Kymlicka, Will. (1995). *Multicultural Citizenship*. Oxford and New York: Oxford University Press.

Kymlicka, Will. (1998). *Finding Our Way*. Oxford and New York: Oxford University Press.

Kymlicka, Will. (2003). "Multicultural States and Intercultural Citizens." *Theory and Research in Education* 1:2.

Laclau, Ernesto. (2001). "Can Immanence Explain Social Struggles?" *Diacritics* 31:4.

Lagueux, Maurice. (2001). *Actualité de la philosophie de l'histoire*. Quebec City: Presses de l'université Laval.

MacIntyre, Alasdair. (1981). *After Virtue: A Study in Moral Theory*. Notre Dame, IN: Notre Dame University Press.

Marx, Karl. (1994). *Selected Writings*, ed. Lawrence H. Simon. Indianapolis, IN: Hackett.

McCarney, Joseph. (2000). *Hegel on History*. London: Routledge.

Oakeshott, Michael. (1975). *On Human Conduct*. Oxford: Clarendon Press.

Parekh, Bhikhu. (2000). *Rethinking Multiculturalism*. Cambridge, MA: Harvard University Press.

Russon, John. (1995). "Hegel, Heidegger, and Ethnicity." *Southern Journal of Philosophy* 33.

Russon, John. (2003). *Human Experience: Philosophy, Neurosis, and the Elements of Everyday Life*. Albany: State University of New York Press.

Serres, Michel. (2001). *Hominescence*. Paris: Le Pommier.

Taylor, Charles. (1994). "The Politics of Recognition," in Amy Gutmann (ed.), *Multiculturalism: Examining the Politics of Recognition*. Princeton, NJ: Princeton University Press.

Todd, Emmanuel. (2003). *After the Empire: The Breakdown of the American Order*. New York: Columbia University Press.

Touraine, Alain. (2000). *Can We Live Together? Equality and Difference*, trans. David Macey. Stanford, CA: Stanford University Press.

Veyne, Paul. (1984). *Writing History: Essay on Epistemology*, trans. Mina Moore-Rinvolcri. Middletown, CT: Wesleyan University Press.

Yegenoglu, Meyda. (2003). "Liberal Multiculturalism and the Ethics of Hospitality in the Age of Globalization." *Postmodern Culture* 13:2.

Index

A

C

D

M

MacIntyre, Alasdair, 35–37, 153

Making It Explicit: Reasoning, Representing, and Discursive Commitment) (Brandom), 4

Marx, Karl

    class struggles, 111–12, 127

    Communist Manifesto, 108, 111, 115, 117, 126–27

    Critique of the Gotha Programme, 115

    dynamics of history, 109, 112–13, 115, 125, 149

    dynamics of social life, 113

    The Eighteenth Brumaire of Louis Bonaparte, 119

    past-present-future complex, 110, 113

    Preface to a Contribution to the Critique of Political Economy, 118

    Selected Writings, 107, 109, 111–12, 114–20, 127, 153

    speculative philosophy of history., 107, 109–10, 115, 121, 130, 144

    struggles of history, 150

    telos of history, 114, 120, 125, 149

    Theses on Feuerbach, 120

    thesis, eleventh, 120

"The Material of its Realization" (Hegel), 91

May, Todd, 147, 151

"The Means of its Realization" (Hegel), 91

Meditations on First Philosophy (Descartes), 101–2, 151

misrecognition, 77, 87–88, 148

modal square, 15–16, 30, 32–33, 37, 48, 51, 91, 94, 116, 149

multicultural

    coexistence, 69, 79

    conflicts, 85

    dimensions of history, 72

    dynamics, 72

    ideal *vs.,* 79

    justice, 82–83

    public spaces, 70–72

    reality, 80

    social life, 113

    societies, 72, 80, 82–83

    space, 100

    world, 3–6, 12, 15–17, 25, 27–28, 45–46, 49, 52–54, 56–57, 68–70, 74–75, 80–82, 84–85, 92–93, 100–101, 107, 126, 135–37, 140–41, 148

"Multicultural States and Intercultural Citizens" (Kymlicka), 69, 82, 153

multiculturalism, 69

Multitude: War in the Age of Empire (Hardt and Negri), 126–31, 133–38, 140–41, 152

mutual recognition, 12, 54, 56, 75, 79, 81, 84, 100–101, 103, 107–8, 124, 148–49. *See also* recognition